DIRECTIONS OF THE BODY IN SPACE

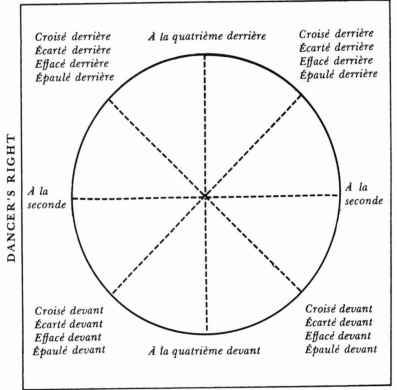

Croisé derrière
Écarté derrière
Effacé derrière
Épaulé derrière

À la quatrième derrière

Croisé derrière
Écarté derrière
Effacé derrière
Épaulé derrière

DANCER'S RIGHT

À la seconde

À la seconde

DANCER'S LEFT

Croisé devant
Écarté devant
Effacé devant
Épaulé devant

À la quatrième devant

Croisé devant
Écarté devant
Effacé devant
Épaulé devant

FRONT OF STAGE

The corners of the square represent the corners of the stage. The dancer is represented by the center of the circle, facing the audience. He can turn and move in any of the given directions in the second or fourth position of the feet. If he moves towards one of the front corners, he will be in either *croisé, écarté, effacé* or *épaulé devant* depending on which foot is front, or whether he is in the second or fourth position, or whether his shoulders are turned. If he moves toward one of the back corners, he will be in either *croisé, écarté, effacé* or *épaulé derrière* for the same reasons. If he moves forward, he will be *à la quatrième devant*, backwards *à la quatrième derrière*. If he moves sideways, he will be *à la seconde*. See entries: Directions of the Body and Positions of the Body.

The Language of Ballet

A DICTIONARY

BY THALIA MARA
ILLUSTRATED BY TINA MACKLER

A DANCE HORIZONS BOOK
Princeton Book Company, Publishers
Princeton, New Jersey

First published in 1966 by World Publishing Company,
Cleveland and New York

Republished in 1987 by Princeton Book Company, Publishers,
P. O. Box 109, Princeton, New Jersey 08542

Library of Congress Catalog Card No. 78-181477

ISBN 87127-144-3 (cloth)
ISBN 87127-037-4 (paper)

Cover illustration: Ballet Rehearsal (La salle de danse).
Edgar Degas, c. 1885, oil on canvas.
Courtesy Yale University Art Gallery, New Haven, CT.
Gift of Duncan Phillips, B.A., 1908

Cover design by Design & Illustration

Printed in the United States of America

Foreword

Although the art of ballet was born in Italy, it found its first real home in France and it was a French ballet master who first codified its technique and set the basic rules and principles that will remain as long as classical ballet endures. French is, therefore, the language of ballet—a universal language in use throughout the world wherever the art is taught. However, because of this very factor of world-wide diffusion, usage has developed many variations. Corruptions by teachers with little knowledge of French have also entered to compound the confusion. It is not unheard of that intense arguments develop between dancers over the name of a step or the correctness of a term.

There is a great need for the standardization of ballet terminology in order that teaching ideas may be more easily transmitted from teacher to student and, even more importantly, that such ideas may flow more freely between teachers of differing schools and countries. This dictionary of ballet terms has been written in an attempt to fill that need.

When the Syllabus Committee of the National Academy of Ballet met to decide on terms to be used in the Graded Syllabus of the Academy, these differences were discussed and the decision made to simplify the terms as much as possible, accepting those terms that are most commonly and widely used and, wherever a difference of opinion occurred, those that are most direct and simple.

v

With this in mind two members of the Committee, Madame Olga Ziceva, Director of the Ziceva Ballet School in San Mateo, California, and Mr. Thomas Armour, Director of the Miami Civic Ballet, set to work to compile a dictionary of terms for the use of Academy members and students.

This dictionary is the outgrowth of that work. I have rewritten, edited, and added to the material. Wherever possible I have tried to give the variations of names by which a step or exercise may be known. It is not a manual for self-instruction. Its explanations are simply the bare details of the composition of an exercise or step in order that identification may be accurate and clear. A few abbreviated biographies are included only because the individuals are referred to in the text. The book is not intended to be an encyclopedia. As a nomenclature or glossary it can serve a useful purpose. It is my hope that teachers and students, as well as interested laymen of my beloved art, will find it a practical guide.

Thalia Mara

A

À (ah). At; to.

ADAGE (ah-DAZH). The French term for the Italian *ad agio* (literally, at ease or leisure). 1. The generic term for a series of exercises involving the movements performed to a slow musical tempo (adagio), utilizing *développés* in all positions, line poses such as *arabesques* and *attitudes*, graceful movements, and controlled *pirouettes*. These exercises always form part of "the class" and are designed to develop strength, balance, grace, and elegance of line in both the male and female dancer. 2. That part of the *pas de deux*, in which the *ballerina*, supported by her cavalier, performs the *enlèvements*, *développés* movements *(sur les pointes)*, *pirouettes*, and balances that exhibit her skill, grace, extension, and brilliance, a display that would be impossible without the assistance of the male partner.

AILES DE PIGEONS (ell dih pee-ZHO*n*). Literally, wings of pigeons. The pigeon-wing step, an *allegro* step in which the dancer leaps off one leg throwing the other leg forward. The legs beat, change, beat again, and the dancer lands on the leg from which he jumped. Also called *pistolet*.

AIR, EN L' (ah*n* LAIR). Literally, in the air. 1. A movement made in the air; for example, *fouetté en l'air*. 2. A raised position of the leg when the working foot is elevated until it is at a 90°, or right angle to the hips.

À LA (ah LAH). To the.

ALLEGRO (ah-LEH-gro). The generic term applied to all light and lively springing movements performed to a brisk, lively musical tempo.

1

ALLONGÉ (ah-loh*n*-ᴢʜᴀʏ), **ALLONGÉE** (ah-loh*n*-ᴢʜᴀʏ). Extended, lengthened, or outstretched, as in *arabesque allongée.*

APLOMB (ah-ᴘʟᴏʜ*n*). The controlled centering of the body with all its members (legs, hips, torso, shoulders, arms, and head) correctly aligned to one another, giving the dancer stability and ease of movement on a vertical plane.

ARABESQUE (ah-rah-ʙᴇꜱᴋ). Among the ancient Moors and Greeks, *arabesque* was a name given to an ornament of fantastic and geometric design. In ballet, the name has been given to one of the basic poses to express the grace and charm of geometric design. Essentially the *arabesque* is a long flowing line made by arching the body and balancing it over one foot with the other leg extended behind. The arms extend the pose to make the longest possible line from finger tips to toe tips; the head must be poised in harmony with the line of the body. The basic pose has an infinite number of variations that may be achieved by changing an arm position or the direction of the body in space. The National Academy of Ballet syllabus lists five basic variations upon which all the others are founded:

Arabesque à deux bras (ah-rah-besk ah duh ʙʀᴀʜ). A profile position, leg nearest audience raised, both arms extended forward with the back arm slightly higher, the head turned to the audience, and the eyes looking out. (If the head is held erect with the eyes looking straight forward, this is the third *arabesque* in the Cecchetti method.)

Arabesque à deux bras

2

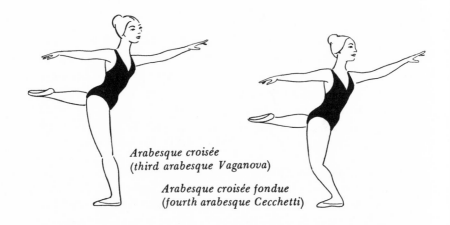

Arabesque croisée
(third arabesque Vaganova)

Arabesque croisée fondue
(fourth arabesque Cecchetti)

Arabesque croisée (ah-rah-besk krwah-ZAY). A three-quarter view of the body, facing a front corner of the stage. In facing the left corner, the left leg is raised and the left arm extended, with the head erect, and the eyes looking straight forward over the left hand. (This is the third *arabesque* in the Vaganova method. If the supporting knee is bent in *demi-plié*, this is the fourth *arabesque* in the Cecchetti method. If the right arm is extended and the head inclined toward the audience, it is the fourth *arabesque*, Vaganova.)

Arabesque croisée à deux bras (ah-rah-besk krwah-zay ah duh BRAH). The same view of the body as in *arabesque*

Arabesque croisée à deux bras

Arabesque croisée à deux bras fondue
(fifth arabesque Cecchetti)

3

croisée. Both arms are extended to the side of the raised leg, with the body and head inclined to the supporting side, the eyes looking to the audience. (If the supporting knee is bent in *demi-plié* and the body and head remain upright as in the *arabesque croisée*, it is the fifth *arabesque* in the Cecchetti method.)

Arabesque épaulée (ah-rah-besk ay-poh-LAY). A profile position as in *arabesque ouverte*, but here the forward arm corresponds to the raised leg and there is a turn of the shoulders so that the back of the dancer may be seen; the head inclines toward the front shoulder, eyes looking at the front hand. (This is the second *arabesque* in both the Cecchetti and Vaganova methods.)

Arabesque épaulée

Arabesque ouverte

Arabesque ouverte (ah-rah-besk oo-VAIRT). A profile position in relation to the audience, with the opposite arm and leg extended in the air (leg nearest audience is raised, arm forward corresponds to supporting leg), head erect, eyes looking straight forward. (This is the first *arabesque* in both the Cecchetti and Vaganova methods.)

4

ARABESQUE. Other variations:

Arabesque allongée (ah-rah-besk ah-lohn-ZHAY). Literally, *arabesque* extended or outstretched. The trunk and arms make a horizontal parallel to the floor, the working leg is raised and stretched as high as possible.

Arabesque allongée

Arabesque allongée à terre (ah-rah-besk ah-lohn-zhay ah TAIR). Literally, *arabesque* extended on the ground. The arms and body are in an *arabesque* position, the leg *pointe tendue derrière,* the supporting knee bent in *plié* at any desired depth from *demiplié* to a low stretched position.

Arabesque à terre (ah-rah-besk ah TAIR). Literally, *arabesque* on the ground. The arms and body are in an *arabesque* position but the leg usually raised is extended behind, *pointe tendue,* on the floor.

Arabesque de face (ah-rah-besk dih FAHss). Literally, *arabesque* facing. An *arabesque* performed facing the audience. The arms may be held in any position.

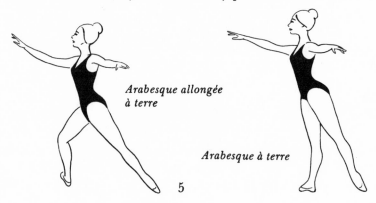

Arabesque allongée à terre

Arabesque à terre

5

Arabesque fondue   *Arabesque ouverte croisée*

Arabesque fondue (ah-rah-besk fohn-DIU). An *arabesque* with the supporting knee bent in a *demi-plié*. Also called *arabesque pliée*.

Arabesque ouverte croisée (ah-rah-besk oo-vairt krwah-ZAY). A profile position, the supporting leg is nearest the audience, the arm forward corresponding to the supporting leg, with the head inclined toward the audience (French school).

Arabesque penchée (ah-rah-besk pahn-SHAY). Literally, *arabesque* leaning. The body leans forward in an oblique line with the head counterbalancing the raised foot, the head low and the foot correspondingly high.

Arabesque penchée

ARRIÈRE, EN (ahn-nah-ree-AIR). Backward. Indicates that a step is taken backward, as in *piqué en arrière*.

ARRONDI (ah-rohn-DEE). Rounded, curved, as in *bras arrondi*.

6

ASSEMBLÉ, PAS (pah-zah-sah*n*-BLAY). Literally, step assembled or assembling step. A basic step of *allegro* ballet work, the *assemblé* is an elevation step in which the dancer brushes one foot outward on the floor into the air and springs vigorously upward with the supporting foot, assembles both feet, and alights in the fifth position with both feet simultaneously. Through usage the term has been shortened to *assemblé*.

Assemblé battu (ah-sah*n*-blay bah-TIU). Literally, beaten assembling step. The *assemblé* begins as above, but the dancer beats the calves of the legs together before assembling the feet and alighting in the fifth position.

Assemblé derrière (ah-sah*n*-blay dih-ree-AIR). Literally, assembled step behind. From the beginning fifth position, the back foot brushes to the second position to make the *assemblé* and returns to its back position in fifth at the close of the step.

Assemblé dessous (ah-sah*n*-blay dih-soo). Literally, assembled step under. From the beginning fifth position, the front foot brushes to the second position to make the *assemblé* and finishes behind the other foot in the fifth position at the close of the step. Also called *assemblé en remontant*.

Assemblé dessus (ah-sah*n*-blay dih-siu). Literally, assembled step over. From the beginning fifth position, the back foot brushes to the second position to make the *assemblé* and finishes in front of the other foot in the fifth position at the close of the step. Also called *assemblé en descendant*.

Assemblé devant (ah-sah*n*-blay dih-vAH*n*). Literally, assembled step before. From the beginning fifth position, the front foot brushes to the second position to make the *assemblé* and returns to its front position in fifth at the close of the step.

Assemblé élancé (ah-sahn-blay ay-lahn-SAY). Literally, assembled step, darting. An *assemblé dessus* which travels to the side. Also called *assemblé porté.*

Assemblé en arrière (ah-sahn-blay ahn-nah-ree-AIR). Literally, assembled step to the back. From the beginning fifth position, the back foot brushes directly backward to make the *assemblé* and returns to its back position in fifth at the close of the step. This step may be performed in place or traveling backward.

Assemblé en avant (ah-sahn-blay ahn-nah-VAHn). Literally, assembled step to the front. From the beginning fifth position, the front foot brushes directly forward to make the *assemblé* and returns to its front position in fifth at the close of the step. This step may be performed in place or traveling forward.

Assemblé en tournant (ah-sahn-blay ahn toor-NAHn). Literally, assembled step turning. An *assemblé dessus* performed with a turn in the air.

Assemblé, petit (p'tee-tah-sahn-BLAY). Literally, small assembled step. This *assemblé* begins with one foot in the air as at the finish of a *jeté.* The supporting foot springs into the air, and both feet close into the fifth position on alighting. There is no brush or opening of the working leg; it drops into the closed position. Also called *assemblé coupé* (Cecchetti method).

Assemblé porté (ah-sahn-blay por-TAY). Literally, assembled step carried. Instead of being performed in place, the *assemblé* travels in any given direction. Also called *assemblé élancé.*

Assemblés de suite (ah-sahn-blay dih SWEET). Literally, steps assembled one after the other. A series of *assemblés* performed in continuity so that the finishing *plié* of one *assemblé* becomes the starting *plié* of the next.

Assemblé soutenu (ah-sahn-blay soo-teh-NIU). Literally, assembled step sustained. The knees are slowly straightened after the final *plié* of each *assemblé*.

Assemblé soutenu en tournant (ah-sahn-blay soo-teh-niu ahn toor-NAHn). Literally, sustained assembled step turning. It may be performed *en tournant en dedans* or *en tournant en dehors*. For *en dedans:* from the beginning fifth position, execute a *rond de jambe à terre en dedans,* with the back foot, closing with a spring to the fifth position front on the *demi-pointes* or *pointes* and follow immediately with a turn *en dedans* on both feet (whole or half turn). Finish in the fifth position´ *demi-plié*. During the turn, change the feet so that the right foot finishes again behind the left in the fifth position. For *en dehors:* reverse all the movements. Execute a *rond de jambe à terre en dehors* with the front foot, closing behind; the turn is *en dehors*. Also called *soutenu en tournant*.

Assemblés sur les pointes (ah-sahn-blay siur lay PWAHNT). Literally, assembled step on the toes. From the beginning fifth position the working foot slides to the second position *pointe tendue à terre* as the supporting knee bends in *demi-plié*. The feet are drawn with a spring to the fifth position on the *pointes* or *demi-pointes*. This step may be performed *dessus, dessous, derrière, devant, en arrière,* and *en avant*.

ATTITUDE (ah-tee-TIUD). A term derived from the Italian *attitudine,* meaning "a way of holding the body." A pose or position in ballet, invented by the Italian school (Carlo

9

Blasis) and suggested by the famous statue of Mercury by sculptor Jean Bologne (1524–1608). There are numerous variations of this pose, which is basically a vertical position of the body supported by one leg, with the other, knee bent, raised behind and the arms in the *troisième en haut* (or *attitude*) position with the raised arm corresponding to the raised leg. The variations also include *attitudes* with the leg raised in front. As with the *arabesque,* the number of variations can be infinite because each change of arm position, turn of the body, lean of the body, and the like can produce a different *attitude*.

Attitude à deux bras

Attitude à deux bras (ah-tee-tiud ah duh BRAH). Literally, attitude with two arms. Also called *attitude en couronne* (French school).

Attitude à terre (ah-tee-tiud ah TAIR). Literally, attitude on the ground. The arms are in the *attitude* position, the body supported on one foot, other foot *pointe tendue* behind, close to supporting ankle.

Attitude croisée (ah-tee-tiud krwah-ZAY). Literally, attitude

Attitude à terre

Attitude croisée (Russian School)

Attitude croisée (Italian School)

Attitude
de face

Attitude
croisée
devant

Attitude
effacée
devant

crossed. The dancer faces a front corner of the stage (*croisé* direction) presenting a three-quarter view of the body to the audience.

Attitude de face (ah-tee-tiud dih FAHSS). Literally, attitude facing. The dancer faces directly forward, presenting a full front view of the body to the audience.

Attitude devant (ah-tee-tiud dih-VAHn). Literally, attitude in front. The arms are in the *attitude* position with the raised leg in front.

Attitude effacée (ah-tee-tiud eh-fah-SAY). Literally, attitude shaded. The dancer faces a front corner of the stage (*effacé* direction), presenting a three-quarter, almost profile, view to the

Attitude effacée
(*Russian School*)

Attitude effacée
(*Italian School*)

11

audience. Also called *attitude ouverte* (French school).

Attitude épaulée (ah-tee-tiud ay-poh-LAY). Literally, attitude shouldered. The dancer faces a corner of the stage (*épaulé* direction) front or back, with the shoulder of the raised arm carried well forward.

Attitude grecque (ah-tee-tiud GREK). Literally, Greek attitude. The dancer assumes *attitude croisée* position with the legs and arms in the fourth position, the body inclined toward side of supporting leg.

Attitude épaulée   *Attitude grecque*

ATTITUDE, EN (ahn-nah-tee-TIUD). Literally, in attitude; i.e., in an *attitude* position. For example, *sauté en attitude, piqué en attitude.*

AVANT, EN (ahn-nah-VAHn). Forward: used to indicate that a step moves forward. For example, *glissade en avant.*

B

BALANCÉ, PAS (pah bah-lahn-SAY). Literally, step rocked, or rocking step. The dancer shifts the weight from one foot to the other. Step with *fondu* on one foot, shift weight to

En balançoire

the ball of the other foot, fall in *fondu* on the first foot. It is executed to three-quarter time, and may be performed *de côté, en avant,* or *en arrière* in any desired direction (*croisé, effacé,* or *de face*).

BALANÇOIRE, EN (ah*n* bah-lah*n*-SWAHR). Literally, like a seesaw. A term applied to a series of *grands battements* that swing like a pendulum forward and backward, passing through the first position each time. The body, too, is part of the swing, so that as the leg goes up the head goes down.

BALLABILE (bah-LAH-bee-lay). An Italian word for a dance performed by a large group of persons, such as a *corps de ballet*.

BALLERINA (bah-lah-REE-nah). An Italian word for "female dancer" (French, *ballerine*): usually used to denote the principal female dancer. *Prima ballerina* is the term for the first principal female dancer of a ballet company.

BALLET (bah-LAY). 1. A specialized form of theatrical dance having its own technique, movements, traditions, and vocabulary. 2. A form of theatrical spectacle combining and fusing ballet dancing, symphonic music, theatrical scenery, costumes, and lighting. The ballet may be a *ballet d'action,* a ballet that tells a dramatic story, tragic or comic, or it may be an abstract or storyless ballet that presents an idea.

13

BALLET BLANC (bah-LAY blah*n*). Literally, white ballet. A ballet (spectacle) in the romantic style deriving from the nineteenth century and often considered the pure classical form of ballet. The costume is the traditional long white ballet skirt.

BALLET CLASSIQUE (bah-lay klah-SEEK). Literally, classical ballet. 1. A style of ballet in which the traditional academic technical form and line are stressed and the emotional content is restricted. 2. A ballet spectacle from traditional repertoire; e.g., *Swan Lake*. (Although *Swan Lake* is a romantic ballet, it is considered part of the classical repertoire.)

BALLET ROMANTIQUE (bah-lay roh-mah*n*-TEEK). 1. A style of ballet in which the academic technical form and line are used poetically to make movement flowing and emotional. 2. A ballet spectacle that tells a story, such as a fairy tale, involving the supernatural.

BALLON (bah-LOH*n*). Literally, ball; bounciness. The light, bounding quality of the ballet dancer when the jump is springy and sustained in the air and the insteps and knees have an elastic quality that gives lightness, softness, and ease to elevation steps.

BALLONNÉ (bah-loh-NAY). Literally, ball-like; bounced. A dance is said to be *ballonné* when it is based on large bounding movements. The French critic, André Levinson, defines *ballonné* as "the *legato* of great *paraboli* described in the air to a waltz movement, or the slow advancing of *développés* in *adagio*, sustained by the singing of the bow."

BALLONNÉ, PAS (pah bah-loh-NAY). Literally, ball step. A spring into the air from one foot while the other executes a *fouetté raccourci*. The step *ballonné* may be performed

14

devant, derrière, or *à la seconde.* It may also be performed *sur la pointe,* when the spring changes to a *relevé* and the musical accent is on the opening of the working leg and the *relevé* of the supporting foot, instead of on the *cou-de-pied* position and the *demi-plié* of the jumped step.

Ballonné à trois temps, pas (pah bah-loh-nay ah trwah TAHn). A *ballonné* step in three movements (Cecchetti method). The step is the same as the *ballonné composé* except that the last movement is a *coupé* instead of closing to the fifth position; i.e., *ballonné, chassé, coupé.* It may be performed *en avant, en arrière,* or *de côté.*

Ballonné composé, pas (pah bah-loh-nay cohn-poh-ZAY). Literally, composite ball step. A compound step consisting of three movements: *ballonné, chassé,* close to the fifth position (French school). It may be performed *en avant, en arrière,* or *de côté.*

BALLOTTÉ, PAS (pah bah-loh-TAY). Literally, tossed step. The step *ballotté* consists of *coupés, dessous* and *dessus,* with the body leaning backward and forward with each change of foot. The step may be performed with *développés* or with straight knees. The direction of the body is usually *effacé.* Also called *jeté bateau* (French school).

BARRE (bahr). Literally, bar. The wooden railing that is fixed horizontally to the wall of the ballet classroom as a hand support in the preliminary exercises of the class. See *Exercices à la barre.*

BAS, EN (ahn BAH). Literally, low. The term indicates a lowered position of the arms, for example, *troisième* or *cinquième position en bas.*

BATTEMENT (baht-MAHn). Literally, beating. A beating action of the leg. There are many types of *battements* covering most of the exercises performed *à la barre.*

15

Battement arrondi (baht-mah*n* ah-roh*n*-DEE). Literally, rounded beating. The working foot describes a *rond de jambe* in the air *en dehors* or *en dedans*. For *en dehors*, extend the working leg forward and carry around in a circular movement to the back, describing an arc in the air with the toes and finishing in the fifth or first position. It may be performed a few inches above the floor, or *à la demi-hauteur*. For *en dedans*, reverse the movement. Also called *battement en rond*.

Battement arrondi, grand (grah*n* baht-mah*n* ah-roh*n*-DEE). Same as *battement arrondi* but performed at 90°, or hip level. Also called *grand battement en rond*.

Battement battu (baht-mah*n* bah-TIU). Literally, beaten beating. The working foot is drawn sharply to the *cou-de-pied* position from an extended position *à la seconde* or *devant* or *derrière*, on the musical accent.

Battement dégagé (baht-mah*n* day-gah-ZHAY). Literally, disengaged beating. An extension of *battement tendu* in which the working foot glides outward on the floor from the fifth or first position, finishes several inches above the floor, and then is brought forcefully down and to the closed position. This movement is usually performed with rapidity to develop the speed and lightness of limb necessary to the dancer. Also called *battement tendu jeté* (Russian school), *battement glissé* (French school).

Battement développé (baht-mah*n* day-vloh-PAY). Literally, developed beating. The term refers to the unfolding of the working leg. From the fifth or first position raise the working foot to the level of the other knee and forcefully unfold it to the farthest extended point in the air, *devant, à la seconde,* or *derrière*. Then return to the fifth or first position as in the *grand battement*.

16

Battement fini piqué, grand (grah*n* baht-mah*n* fee-nee pee-KAY). See *Battement ouvert, grand.*

Battement fondu (baht-mah*n* fohn-DIU). Literally, beating sinking down. An exercise combining *développé* of the working foot with a *demi-plié* of the supporting leg. It may be performed with or without *relevé,* and *à terre* and *en l'air.* Raise the working foot to the *cou-de-pied* position as the supporting knee bends; straighten both knees simultaneously while unfolding the working foot into a *développé, devant, derrière,* or *à la seconde.* The movement may culminate on the *demi-pointe* with a rising *relevé* of the supporting foot, or on the whole foot.

Battement fouetté (baht-mah*n* fweh-TAY). Literally, whipped beating. From an extended second position *en l'air,* draw the working foot sharply back to a pointed position in front or in back of the ankle of the supporting foot, striking the floor with the toes as the foot goes inward. It may also be performed without striking the floor.

Battement frappé (baht-mah*n* frah-PAY). Literally, struck (or striking) beating. From the *cou-de-pied* position, thrust the working foot forcefully outward to an extended position, a few inches above the floor, *devant, à la seconde,* or *derrière,* with the ball of the foot brushing on the floor as it moves outward. *Battement frappé piqué* (or *battement frappé pointé*) is the same exercise performed without brushing the floor but finishing with the toes on the floor.

Battement glissé (baht-mah*n* glee-SAY). Literally, glided beating. See *Battement dégagé.*

Battement, grand (grah*n* baht-MAH*n*). Literally, large beating. The *grand battement* is an extension of the *battement tendu,* beginning in the same way, but from the extended position throw the working leg forcefully into the air to

17

a level of 90° or above, then bring it downward, with control, finishing, as the *battement tendu,* in the fifth or first position. Also called *grand battement jeté* (Russian school).

Battement jeté, grand (grah*n* baht-mah*n* zheh-TAY). See *Battement, grand.*

Battement jeté pointé, grand (grah*n* baht-mah*n* zheh-tay pwahn-TAY). See *Battement ouvert, grand.*

Battement ouvert, grand (grah*n* baht-mah*n* OO-VAIR). Literally, big beating open. A *grand battement* that finishes in an open position *pointe tendue (devant, derrière,* or *à la seconde).* Also called *grand battement fini piqué* (French school), *grand battement jeté pointé* (Russian school).

Battement, petit (p'tee baht-MAH*n*). Literally, small beating. 1. Another term for the *battement tendu.* 2. Any small beating action of the leg or foot as, for example, *petits battements sur le cou-de-pied.*

Battement piqué (baht-mah*n* pee-KAY). Literally, pricked beatings. The working leg is extended *pointe tendue,* lifted lightly, lowered—striking the toes to the floor—and lightly bounced up. It may be performed *devant, à la seconde,* or *derrière.*

Battement raccourci, grand (grah*n* baht-mah*n* rah-koor-SEE). Literally, large beating shortened. The working leg makes a *grand battement* and is sharply drawn back to the knee on the musical accent, then lowered to the fifth or first position. It may be performed *devant, à la seconde,* or *derrière.*

Battement relevé (baht-mah*n* rih-leh-VAY). See *Battement tendu relevé.*

Battement retiré (baht-mah*n* rih-tih-RAY). Literally, withdrawn beatings. The working foot is drawn sharply upward from the fifth or first position to a point at the side of the knee of the supporting leg and returns to a closed position. The thigh is pressed strongly outward to the second position when the leg is raised.

Battements battus, petits (p'tee baht-mah*n* bah-TIU). The working foot makes continuous rapid tiny beats against the front or the back of the supporting instep.

Battements en balançoire (baht-mah*n* ah*n* bah-lah*n*-SWAHR). See *Balançoire, en.*

Battements en cloche (baht-mah*n* ah*n* KLOHSH). Literally, beatings like a bell. The term is used to describe the action of the working leg, which swings back and forth like the clapper of a bell. Pass the working foot through the first position, on each swing extending to a pointed position in the air *devant* and *derrière*. The action of the working leg is like that in *balançoire,* but the body remains upright and motionless as the leg swings.

Battements en cloche, grands (grah*n* baht-mahn-zah*n* KLOHSH). Same as *battements en cloche* but the leg extends at 90° or above.

Battement soutenu (baht-mah*n* soo-teh-NIU). Literally, sustained beating. Extend the working foot from the fifth or first position, *devant, à la seconde,* or *derrière* (with or without a small *développé*), at the same time bending the supporting knee in a *demi-plié.* Then slide the working foot into the closed position while straightening the supporting knee. It may also be performed with a *relevé.* On the close, raise the supporting foot to the *demi-pointe* while drawing in the working foot. The finish is in the fifth or first position on the *demi-pointes.*

19

Battements serrés (baht-mah*n* seh-RAY). Literally, tightened beatings. See *Battements sur le cou-de-pied, petits.*

Battements sur le cou-de-pied, petits (p'tee baht-mah*n* siur lih koo-dih-pee-AY). Literally, small beatings on the ankle. The working foot makes a continuous brushing in-and-out action from front to back and back to front around the ankle of the supporting leg. Also called *battements serrés* (French school).

Battement tendu (baht-mah*n* tah*n*-DIU). Literally, stretched beating. Glide the working leg outward on the floor from a closed position (fifth, third, or first) to an extended, tautly pointed position *devant, à la seconde,* or *derrière* and return to the closed position in the same manner. It may be performed with tightly pulled-up knees or with a *demi-plié* on the return to the closed position.

Battement tendu jeté (baht-mah*n* tah*n*-diu zheh-TAY). See *Battement dégagé.*

Battment tendu relevé (baht-mah*n* tah*n*-diu rih-leh-VAY). Literally, stretched beating relifted. Glide the working leg outward on the floor from a closed position (fifth, third, or first) to an extended, tautly pointed position, *devant, à la seconde,* or *derrière;* then, working through the instep, lower the heel of the working foot to the floor and quickly raise again, after which glide it back to the closed position. The weight may be shifted as the heel is lowered or kept over the supporting leg; however, if the weight is not shifted, there will be a displacement of the hips as the heel is lowered. Both ways of performing the movement are taught.

BATTERIE (bah-TREE). Literally, battery. The generic term for all allegro steps in which the legs beat against

each other in the air. *Batterie* is divided into two categories
—*grande* and *petite*—according to the elevation of the
step.

Batterie, grande (grahnd bah-TREE). Literally, large beating. The collective term for the steps of high elevation in
which the legs beat against each other, for example, *cabriole, entrechat six de volée.*

Batterie, petite (p'teet bah-TREE). Literally, small beating.
The collective term for the small, quick, beaten steps of
allegro that are performed with small elevation, for example, *brisé, royale, entrechat quatre.*

BATTU (bah-TIU). Beaten, as in *jeté battu, assemblé battu.*

BEAT. See *Battement.*

BEAUCHAMP, PIERRE (pyair bo-SHAn), 1639—1705.
French Dancing Master to King Louis XIV. One of the
original members of the group to whom Louis XIV gave
the charter for establishing the first known academy of
dancing, known as the Academie Royale de la Danse, in
Paris, France. In 1671 he became Maître de Ballet at the
Academie. He named the five positions of the feet upon
which all movements are based, and laid down the precepts which form the basis of technical virtuosity. He was
the first to codify the dance.

BLASIS, CARLO (KAHR-low BLAH-sees), 1803—1878. Italian-
born dancer, choreographer, teacher, and the founder of
the Italian school of ballet technique. Blasis, the scion of
a noble family, received an exceptionally fine education
in the arts, in mathematics, anatomy, and literary studies.
He made his debut as a dancer at an early age and achieved
great success. During his dancing career he was greatly

21

influenced by Dauberval (the pupil of Noverre, and Pierre Gardel who was the ballet master at the Opéra in Paris in the latter part of the eighteenth century, and the early part of the nineteenth). In the early 1830s at the height of his dancing career he was forced to retire due to a leg injury. In 1837 Blasis was made Director of the Imperial Ballet Academy in Milan with his wife, Annunziata (his pupil and dancing partner), as Co-Director. During his directorate, the Academy, which was connected with La Scala, the Royal Opera, became the leading dancing academy of the world and up to recent times has sent teachers all over the globe to spread the Italian technique. Blasis' books *An Elementary Treatise upon the Theory and Practice of the Art of Dancing,* published in 1820, and *The Code of Terpsichore,* published in 1830, were the first comprehensive books on dancing technique, as it is understood today, to appear in print. They influenced ballet academies and teachers throughout the world. Blasis' construction of "the lesson," beginning with the exercises at the *barre* and the division of center work into sections of *port de bras,* center exercises, adagio, pirouettes, and allegro, remain the basis of every ballet dancer's training today. The fundamentals laid down by him are unchanged and the ideals and traditions established during his directorate at the Imperial Academy in Milan still live in every true ballet school. See *Italian school.*

BOURNONVILLE, AUGUST (oh-GOOST BOOR-non-vee-yih), 1805–1879. Dancer, choreographer, teacher, born in France, who worked mainly in Denmark. He studied first under his father, Antoine Bournonville, French dancer and choreographer, who was a pupil of Noverre. Later he studied under Auguste Vestris and other great French teachers. He followed his father as choreographer of the Royal Danish Ballet from 1829 to 1877. See *Russian school.*

BRAS (brah). Arm.

BRAS, À DEUX (a duh BRAH). Literally, with two arms. A position of the arms in which they are extended as for *arabesque* (palms down) with the back arm raised a little higher than the front arm. Both elbows are slightly bent. See illustrations for *arabesque à deux bras* and *arabesque croisée à deux bras*.

BRAS AU REPOS (brah-zoh rih-POH). Literally, arms at ease. A preparatory position of the arms in which they are held at the sides in a rounded position, with the finger tips touching the thighs (French school). It corresponds to the *première position* of the National Academy of Ballet and the Cecchetti method. See *Bras, positions de.*

BRAS BAS (brah BAH). Literally, arms low or arms down. The arms are held down in front of the body and are rounded to form a circle (French school). It corresponds to the *cinquième position en bas* of the National Academy of Ballet and the Cecchetti method. See *Bras, positions de.*

BRAS CROISÉ (brah krwah-ZAY). Literally, arms in a crossed position. The arms are held at a midway position, with one arm curved in front of the body and the other extended at the side in the second position (French school). It corresponds to the *troisième position en avant* of the National Academy of Ballet and the *quatrième position en avant* of the Cecchetti method. See *Bras, positions de.*

BRAS, DEMI (d'mee BRAH). Literally, half arms or arms at the halfway position. The arms are held at a position midway between the *cinquième en avant* (National

Demi bras

23

Academy of Ballet and the Cecchetti method) and *à la seconde,* with the palms turned upward (French school).

BRAS EN ATTITUDE (brah-zahn-nah-tee-TIUD). Literally, arms in the attitude position. It corresponds to the *troisième en haut* of the National Academy of Ballet. See *Bras, positions de.*

BRAS EN COURONNE (brah-zahn koo-ROHn). Literally, arms in the shape of a crown. The arms are held up in a rounded position to form a circle slightly forward of the head (French school). It corresponds to the *cinquième position en haut* of the National Academy of Ballet and the Cecchetti method. It is the *cinquième position* of the French school. See *Bras, positions de.*

BRAS, POSITIONS DE (poh-zee-syon dih BRAH). Literally, positions of the arms. The basic positions of the arms from which all ballet arm movements emanate. Although the positions themselves are standard throughout the world, the method of naming and numbering them differs in the various schools, i.e., French, Italian (or Cecchetti), and Russian. The French school uses a standard of a preparatory and five basic positions. The Cecchetti method standard includes nine basic positions (five, with three variations of the fifth position and two of the fourth position, plus the *demi-seconde* position). The Russian school generally accepts the standard French positions, but the Vaganova method, in use today, lists a standard of a preparatory and three basic positions. Although it seems that the Cecchetti method has a larger number of basic positions, all these positions are known and used in all

Première

Seconde

Troisième en bas

Troisième en avant

Troisième en haut

Quatrième

Cinquième en bas

Cinquième en avant

Cinquième en haut

Demi-seconde

25

schools. The National Academy of Ballet, in its syllabus, has incorporated all of these positions into a standard consisting of ten basic positions. Illustrated are the National Academy of Ballet standard positions of the arms. In these illustrations the *première* position is called preparatory position in the French school; the *troisième en avant* is the *quatrième en avant* of the Cecchetti method; the *troisième en haut* is the *quatrième en haut,* Cecchetti; the *cinquième en bas* is called *bras bas* in the French school; the *cinquième en avant* is the *première position* in both the French school and Vaganova method; the *cinquième en haut* is the *troisième,* Vaganova method.

BRAVURA (brah-voo-rah). With spirit and boldness of execution.

BRISÉ, PAS (pah bree-ZAY). Literally, step broken; breaking step. An allegro step of the *petite batterie.* The step *brisé* may be performed *dessus* and *dessous.*

Brisé dessous (bree-zay dih-SOO). Literally, breaking step under. From the fifth position *demi-plié* the front foot makes a *dégagé à la seconde,* crosses under, and beats in back of the supporting leg as the calves strike together and the dancer springs into the air. The front foot then returns to its original position.

Brisé dessus (bree-zay dih-SIU). Literally, breaking step over. From the fifth position *demi-plié* the back foot makes a *dégagé à la seconde,* crosses over, and beats in front of the supporting leg as the calves strike together and the dancer springs into the air. The back foot then returns to its original position, behind, in the fifth position *demi-plié.*

BRISÉ VOLÉ, PAS (pah bree-zay voh-LAY). Literally, breaking step flying. The dancer beats the legs as in the step *brisé* but finishes on one foot instead of on both feet. The step *brisé volé* is performed *en avant* and *en arrière*. There are three accepted but differing methods of executing the *brisé volé*.

Brisé volé en arrière (bree-zay voh-lay ahn-nah-ree-AIR). Literally, breaking step flying backward. 1. From the fifth position *demi-plié*, make a *dégagé à la seconde* with the front foot, cross under, and beat in back of the supporting leg with the calves striking together while springing into the air. Then return this same foot to the floor, *fondu* while the other foot finishes pointed *sur le cou-de-pied* (knee bent) *derrière*. 2. The beat may be performed in the same manner but the raised leg remains straight at the finish of the step instead of bending after the beat. 3. A *rond de jambe en dehors* with straight knee may precede the beat instead of the *dégagé*.

Brisé volé en avant (bree-zay voh-lay ahn-nah-VAHn). Literally, breaking step flying forward. 1. From the fifth position, make a *dégagé à la seconde* with the back foot, cross over, and beat in front of the supporting leg with the calves striking together while springing into the air. Then return this same foot to the floor, finishing *fondu* while the other foot finishes *sur le cou-de-pied devant*. 2. The beat may be performed in the same manner but the raised leg remains straight at the finish of the step instead of bending after the beat. 3. A *rond de jambe en dedans* with straight knee may precede the beat instead of the *dégagé*.

Brisé télémaque (bree-zay tay-lay-MAHK). A particular *enchaînement* of *petite batterie* that includes *brisés*. This is a very old tradition passed on by dancers from generation to generation. The name probably derives from an old

27

ballet, *Télémaque dans l'Ile de Calypso,* produced in 1790 at the Paris Opéra, for which this *enchaînement* was composed by Pierre Gardel, one of the founding fathers of the art of ballet. Many versions exist today. Originally the *enchaînement* was performed to three-quarter time, but another in four-quarter time appeared many years ago. Following is the *brisé télémaque* as taught by Olga Preobrajenskaya. *Brisé télémaque* (three-quarter time): *Brisé dessus, entrechat quatre, entrechat trois derrière, brisé dessus, entrechat quatre, entrechat cinq devant, brisé dessous, entrechat quatre, entrechat trois devant, brisé dessous, entrechat quatre, entrechat trois derrière. Brisé télémaque* (four-quarter time): *Brisé dessus, brisé dessous, entrechat quatre, entrechat trois derrière, brisé dessus, brisé dessous, entrechat quatre, entrechat cinq devant, brisé dessous, brisé dessus, entrechat quatre, entrechat trois devant, brisé dessous, brisé dessus, entrechat quatre, entrechat trois derrière.*

𝒞

CABRIOLE (kah-bree-OHL). Literally, caper, derived from the Italian *capriola,* a goatlike leap. An allegro step of *grande batterie.* The *cabriole* is a flying movement in which one leg is thrown into the air, while the supporting leg is brought forcefully to meet it, beating against it and thrusting it higher in the air. *Cabrioles* are performed *devant, derrière,* and *à la seconde,* in any given position of the body, i.e., *croisé, écarté, effacé,* or *épaulé.* They may be finished *ouverte* or *fermée.*

Cabriole à la seconde (kah-bree-ohl ah lah seh-GOHND). Literally, caper to the second position. *Cabriole à la seconde* follows the same principle as the *cabriole devant* and *derrière.* The opening leg may come from either the front or the back, depending on the preceding step.

Cabriole derrière (kah-bree-ohl dih-ree-AIR). Literally, caper behind. It may be performed in a *croisé, effacé,* or *épaulé* direction. The position of the body is *arabesque.* *Demi-plié* in the fifth position, throw the back leg backward and upward, spring after it, raising the supporting leg to meet the raised leg, beat the calves forcefully together sending the top leg higher into the air, both knees straight in the beat, descend *fondu* on supporting foot. The finish of the step depends on whether the *cabriole* is *ouverte* or *fermée.* If *ouverte,* the leg remains in the air; if *fermée,* the leg closes to the fifth position *demi-plié.*

Cabriole devant (kah-bree-ohl dih-VAHn). Literally, caper in front. It may be performed in a *croisé* or *effacé* direction. *Demi-plié* in the fifth position, throw the back leg forward and upward, spring after it, raising the supporting leg to meet the raised leg, beat the calves forcefully together, sending the top leg higher into the air, both knees straight in the beat, descend *fondu* on supporting foot. The finish of the step depends on whether the *cabriole* is *ouverte* or *fermée.* If *ouverte,* the leg remains in the air; if *fermée,* the leg closes to the fifth position *demi-plié.*

Cabriole fermée (kah-bree-ohl fair-MAY). Literally, caper closed. After the beating of the legs, alight on one foot (the original supporting foot) and quickly close the working foot into the fifth position.

Cabriole fouetté (kah-bree-ohl fweh-TAY). Literally, caper whipped. Perform a *cabriole devant* followed immediately by a *fouetté en l'air.* Also called *fouetté battu.*

Cabriole italienne (kah-bree-ohl ih-tahl-ee-EHN). Literally, Italian caper. A variation of the *cabriole fouetté* in which the dancer first performs the *fouetté en l'air,* finishing with the *cabriole* in *arabesque.*

Cabriole ouverte (kah-bree-ohl oo-VAIRT). Literally, caper open. After the beating of the legs, alight on one foot (the original supporting foot), holding the working leg in the air in any desired pose, for example, *arabesque, effacé, devant,* etc.

CAMBRÉ (kah*n*-BRAY). Literally, arched. The backward or sideways bending of the body from the waist.

CARACTÈRE, DANSE DE (dah*n*s dih kah-rahk-TAIR). See *Danse de caractère.*

CARRÉ, EN (ah*n* kah-RAY). Literally, in the shape of a square. A term used to indicate that a step or *enchaînement* is to be performed in the shape of a square. Also called *en quarré.*

CAVALIER (kav-ah-LEER). The male partner of the ballerina.

CECCHETTI, ENRICO (on-REE-koh cheh-KEH-tee), 1850–1928. He was born in Rome, the son of Cesare Cecchetti, leading dancer and ballet master, and Serafina, a *prima ballerina.* Cecchetti was actually born in the Tordinona Theater and made his public debut as a dancer at the age of five in the ballet, *Il Jocatore.* Shortly thereafter he and his parents were members of the first Italian ballet troupe to tour America. At the age of thirteen he was enrolled in the École de Danse in Florence to study under Giovanni Lepri who was a pupil of the great Carlo Blasis (see *Blasis, Carlo*). At nineteen he made his formal debut on the stage of La Scala, Milan. He toured Italy and all of Europe as a star dancer for some years thereafter. In the summer of 1874 he made his first appearance in Russia at a popular summer music hall on the outskirts of St. Petersburg. He created a sensation with his "amazing virtuosity." The press referred to him as "that bone-splitting specialist of vertiginous dexterity." He was invited to teach at the Imperial School and became, for many years, one of the most prominent figures in the ballet world in St. Petersburg. In 1902 he became the director of the Imperial School of Ballet at Warsaw for a brief period. For some years he toured the world with Anna Pavlova as her ballet master. From 1909 until 1918 he was associated with the Diaghilev Ballet as both teacher of its star performers and performing artist in mime roles. From 1918 until 1923 Cecchetti taught in London, where he opened a private school. In 1923 he returned to Italy and in 1925 became ballet master at La Scala Opera House in Milan where he remained actively teaching until his death. See *Russian school.*

CECCHETTI METHOD (cheh-KEH-tee). A system of teaching devised by students of Maestro Enrico Cecchetti, in England, based on the exercises and *enchaînements* presented in his classes.

CENTER PRACTICE. See *Exercices au milieu.*

CHAÎNÉS, TOURS (toor sheh-NAY). Literally, chains; links. A series of small turning steps performed continuously in rapid succession; the performer makes a half turn on each foot. It may be performed in a straight line or circling the stage. Also called *déboulés* and *petits tours.*

CHANGEMENT BATTU (shah*n*zh-mah*n* bah-TIU). Literally, beaten change. The calves of the legs are beaten against each other before the change of feet in the air. Usually called *royale.*

CHANGEMENT DE PIEDS (shah*n*zh-mah*n* dih pee-AY). Literally, change of feet. From the fifth position, *demi-plié,* spring into the air, change the feet in the air, and finish in fifth position *demi-plié. Changement de pieds* may be performed *grand* (high jump into the air) or *petit* (small jump). In *grand changement de pieds* (Cecchetti method), the knees are drawn upward on the jump so

31

that in the air the dancer brings the soles of the feet together, drawing them well upward. The term *changement de pieds* is usually shortened to *changement*.

CHANGER DE PIED (shah*n*-zhay dih pee-ᴀʏ). Literally, to change one's foot. Indicates either a change of foot from a front position to a back position (as in *échappé, changer de pied*), or a change of weight from one foot to the other.

CHANGER, SANS (sah*n* shah*n*-ᴢʜᴀʏ). Literally, without changing. Indicates that the feet do not change places during the execution of a step but will finish in their original positions, for example, *échappé à la seconde sans changer*.

CHARACTER DANCE. See *Danse de caractère*.

CHASSÉ, PAS (pah shah-ꜱᴀʏ). Literally, chasing step. The name of the step indicates the action of the feet when the step is performed in a series. One foot seems to chase the other foot out of its position. *Chassés* may be performed *en avant, en arrière*, and *de côté*, in *croisé, écarté, effacé*, or *épaulé* directions. To perform a *chassé en avant*, from the fifth position *demi-plié*, spring upward into the air alighting *fondu* on the back foot, with the front foot arched *sur le cou-de-pied devant;* slide the raised foot forward on the floor to the fourth position, draw the back foot to the front foot, springing into the air in fifth position, repeat the slide, etc. Reverse the movement to make the *chassé en arrière*. Use the same principle for *chassé de côté*, cutting under (i.e., behind) each time. Also called *temps levé chassé* (Cecchetti method).

Chassé (shah-ꜱᴀʏ), **Chassée** (shah-ꜱᴀʏ), Cecchetti method. A gliding step on the floor from a closed position to an open one. *Demi-plié* fifth position, slide one foot outward to the fourth or second position (depending on whether the *chassé* is *en avant, en arrière*, or *à la seconde*), keeping the weight equalized over both feet and remaining in the *demi-plié;* straighten both knees, stretching the other foot *pointe tendue.* It may be performed in any given direction and pose of the body, as for example, *croisé derrière, croisé devant, arabesque, effacé, à la seconde,* etc. The step may be concluded by holding the open position or closing the extended foot into the fifth position.

Chassé en tournant (shah-say ah*n* toor-NAH*n*). Literally, chased step turning. Execute a *tour en l'air,* alighting on one foot and *chassé* forward. If a series of *chassés en tournant* is being performed, immediately close the back foot to the fifth position behind and repeat the *tour en l'air,* etc. Otherwise, the finish of the step will be dictated by the step following.

Chassé passé en avant (shah-say pah-say ah*n*-nah-VAH*n*). Literally, chasing step passing forward. The *chassé* movement is performed by sliding the back foot through the first position to the fourth position in front.

CHOREGRAPHE (kor-eh-GRAHF). The French word for "choreographer," derived from the Greek *choreia,* dance, and *graphos,* writer. One who composes dances and ballets. Originally, in the eighteenth century, the word was used to denote a person who recorded ballets or dances by a system of dance notation.

CHOREGRAPHIE (kor-eh-grah-FEE). Derived from the Greek *choreia,* dance, and *graphia,* writing. Choreography; a dance composition. Originally, in the eighteenth century, the art of dance notation.

CHOREOGRAPHER. See *Choregraphe.*

CHOREOGRAPHY. Dance composition, including movement, time (music), space, and floor patterns or designs.

CINQ (sa*n*k). Five, as in *entrechat cinq.*

CINQUIÈME (san-KYEM). Fifth, as in *cinquième position*.

CISEAUX (see-ZOH). Literally, scissors. A scissorslike movement made by opening the legs to a wide position (either second or fourth) in the air.

CISEAUX, PAS DE (pah dih see-ZOH). Literally, scissors step. This term applies to two different steps. 1. Execute a *grand battement devant* with the right leg, then spring immediately into the air executing a *grand battement devant* with the left leg (the legs pass each other with straight knees); alight *fondu* on the right, executing a *grand battement* in *balançoire* with the left leg. The finishing pose is in *arabesque fondue*. 2. From the fifth position, *demi-plié*, spring straight upward into the air, opening both legs as in *grand battement*. This may be performed facing the audience obliquely (*effacé*) and opening the legs to the fourth position, or facing straight (*de face*), opening the legs to the second position. Finish with *fondu* in the fifth position.

CLOCHE, EN (ahn KLOHSH). Literally, like a bell. See *Battements en cloche*.

COLLÉ (koh-LAY). Literally, adhering; glued. A term indicating that the legs are to be held tightly together in the air in a jump.

COMPOSÉ, PAS (pah kohn-poh-ZAY). A composed or compound step consisting of several movements or steps. Examples are the *sissonne retombée* and *ballonné composé*.

CONTRETEMPS (kohn-treh-TAHn). Literally, against time. Counter beat. 1. A compound step (*pas composé*), consisting of *coupé dessus* (*demi-pointe*), *tombé en avant*, close to the fifth position in the back, remaining in the *plié*. It is executed very quickly prior to the beat of the music. 2. In the Cecchetti method, the *contretemps* is also a compound step consisting of two parts: first, the *coupé, tombé, fermé* as above, followed immediately by *temps levé, chassé croisé en avant.*

CORPS (kor). Body.

CORPS DE BALLET (kor dih bah-LAY). Literally, body of the ballet. The group of dancers that comprise the mass of the ballet company. Its members dance as a group and form the background for the soloists.

CÔTÉ, DE (dih koh-TAY). Sideways. Indicates that a step is to be performed to the side, right or left.

COU-DE-PIED (koo-dih-pee-AY). Literally, neck of the foot. The instep.

    Cou-de-pied, sur le (siur lih koo-dih-pee-AY). Literally, on the instep. *Sur le cou-de-pied devant* denotes a position in which the working foot embraces the ankle of the supporting foot, being cupped around it. The heel of the working foot presses forward, the toes press backward as far as possible, the instep encircles the anklebone of the supporting foot. *Sur le cou-de-pied derrière* denotes a position in which the working foot is cupped in the same way but is held behind the ankle with the toes pressing away from the supporting heel.

COUPÉ (koo-PAY). Literally, cut; cutting. A step is said to be *coupé* when it is shortened, for example, *assemblé coupé* (Cecchetti method).

COUPÉ, PAS (pah koo-PAY). Literally, cutting step. One foot cuts the other away and takes its place. *Coupés* may be performed with a jump or with a *relevé.* Sometimes *coupé* refers to a step in an *enchaînement,* sometimes merely to a movement for a change of feet.

    Coupé ballotté (koo-pay bah-loh-TAY). Literally, cutting step tossed. A series of *coupés dessous* and *dessus* performed

35

with a leaning of the body in a rocking movement. See *Ballotté, pas.*

Coupé brisé (koo-pay bree-ZAY). Literally, cutting broken step. A *pas composé,* or compound step, consisting of a *coupé dessous* and a *brisé volé en arrière.*

Coupé chassé en tournant (koo-pay shah-say ahn toor-NAHn). Literally, cutting chasing step turning. A *pas composé,* or compound step, consisting of a *coupé dessous en tournant* and a *chassé en avant.* The step is performed rapidly with the body leaning in the direction of the step. It may also be performed with a *rond de jambe en dedans* into a *coupé dessus en tournant* before the *chassé.*

Coupé dessous (koo-pay dih-soo). Literally, cutting step under. The working foot cuts under the heel of the supporting foot, replacing it. It may also be performed *en tournant,* turning one turn in the air.

Coupé dessus (koo-pay dih-SIU). Literally, cutting step over. The working foot cuts over the toes of the supporting foot, replacing it. It may also be performed *en tournant.*

Coupé en tournant (koo-pay ahn toor-NAHn). See *Coupé dessous* and *Coupé dessus.*

Coupé fouetté raccourci (koo-pay fweh-tay rah-koor-SEE). Literally, cutting step, whipped, shortened. A *pas composé,* or compound step, consisting of a *coupé dessous* and a *fouetté raccourci,* usually performed *sur les pointes.*

Coupé jeté en tournant (koo-pay zheh-tay ahn toor-NAHn). Literally, cutting thrown step, turning. A *pas composé,* or compound step, consisting of a *coupé dessous* with a complete turn and a *grand jeté en avant* into an *attitude* position. These are usually performed in a series and may be done *sur place, en diagonal,* or *en manège.* Also called *tour de reins.*

COURONNE, EN (ahn koo-ROHn). Literally, crownwise; in the shape of a crown. Describing the *cinquième position en haut* of the arms. See *Bras, positions de.*

COURU (koo-RIU). Running, as in *pas couru, pas de bourrée couru.*

CROISÉ (krwah-ZAY), **CROISÉE** (krawh-ZAY). Literally, crossed. A particular placing of the body in space as seen from the audience. The dancer stands at an oblique angle to the audience, presenting a three-quarter view of the body, with the appearance of one leg crossing over the other. See also *Directions of the body, Positions of the body,* and frontispiece diagram.

Croisé derrière (krwah-zay dih-ree-AIR). Literally, crossed in back. The dancer stands at an oblique angle to the audience, with the foot farthest from the audience opened to the fourth position back, *à terre* or *en l'air.*

Croisé devant (krwah-zay dih-VAHn). Literally, crossed in front. The dancer stands at an oblique angle to the audience with the foot nearest the audience opened to the fourth position front, *à terre* or *en l'air.*

Croisé derrière   *Croisé devant*

Croisé en arrière (krwah-zay ahn-nah-ree-AIR). Literally, crossing backward. A direction in space when executing a step. It indicates that the step will be performed diagonally, with the working foot farthest from the audience crossed under the supporting foot, as, for example, in *chassé croisé en arrière.*

Croisé en avant (krwah-zay ahn-nah-VAHn). Literally, crossing forward. A direction in space when executing a step. It indicates that the step will be performed diagonally, with the working foot nearest the audience crossed over the supporting foot, as, for example, in *chassé croisé en avant.*

CROIX, EN (ahn KRWAH). Literally, crosswise; in the shape of a cross. It indicates that an exercise is to be performed successively *à la quatrième devant, à la seconde, à la quatrième derrière,* or vice versa. For example, *battements tendus en croix.*

𝒟

DANSE (dahns). Dance.

DANSE COMIQUE (dahns koh-MEEK). Literally, comical dance. The term actually refers to popular dance, or dance of the people, rather than comical dance. A term of the eighteenth and nineteenth centuries for what we now call *danse de caractère* (character dancing).

DANSE DE CARACTÈRE (dahns dih kah-rahk-TAIR). Literally, dance of character, or character dancing. 1. The generic term for all theater dance founded on folk or national dances. 2. A dance based on the movements associated with a particular profession, trade, occupation, type of personality, etc.; for example, shoemaker's dance, shepherd's dance, gossip's dance.

DANSE DE DEMI-CARACTÈRE (dahns dih d'mee-kah-rahk-TAIR). Literally, semicharacter dancing. The generic term applied to dances of a special character, or having characteristics of national styles of movement, but which, however, are based on the technique of the classical ballet. Two examples are: the swans in the ballet *Swan Lake,* and the peasants in the ballet *Giselle.*

DANSE NOBLE (dahns NOH-blih). Literally, noble dance. The purely classic style of ballet, the characteristics of which are nobility, elegance, grace, majesty, poise, and the like. An example is the *grand pas de deux* in *The Sleeping Beauty.*

DANSEUR (dahn-SUHR). Male dancer.

DANSEUR NOBLE (dahn-suhr NOH-blih). Literally, noble dancer. A male dancer who excels in the noble style of ballet.

DANSEUR, PREMIER (prehm-YAY dahn-SUHR). First male dancer. A principal male dancer in a ballet company.

DANSEUSE (dahn-SUHZ). Female dancer.

DANSEUSE, PREMIÈRE (prehm-YAIR dahn-SUHZ). First female dancer. A principal female dancer in a ballet company.

DAUBERVAL, JEAN (zhahn doh-behr-VAHL), 1742–1806. French ballet dancer and choreographer, student and disciple of Noverre. He did much to forward the ideas of his master, producing many ballets in Marseilles. He was famous for his comedy ballets. One, *La Fille Mal Gardée,* still exists in present-day repertoire although the choreography is not his but that of later choreographers. See *Russian school.*

DÉBOÎTÉ, PAS (pah deh-bwah-TAY). Literally, disjoined step; disjoining step. An *emboîté sur les pointes* when it is executed *en arrière*. The working foot opens from the fifth position front, on *pointes* or *demi-pointes,* and closes to the fifth position back, remaining on the *pointes* or *demi-pointes.* Also called *emboîté en reculant* (French school).

DÉBOULÉS (day-boo-LAY). Literally, rollings like a ball. A series of turns performed in a straight line or in a circle, with very quick half turns on each foot, the feet remaining in the first position, on the *pointes* or *demi-pointes* (French school). Also called *chaînes* and *petits tours.*

DEDANS, EN (ahn dih-DAHn). Literally, inward. 1. A term used to indicate that a movement originates in the back and circles toward the front, for example, *rond de jambe en dedans.* 2. A term used to indicate that in a *pirouette* the turn is made in the direction of the supporting foot; that is, if the turn is made on the right foot, it will be to the right.

DÉGAGÉ, PAS (pah day-gah-zHAY). Literally, disengaged or disengaging step. A pointing of the fully arched foot to an open position *à terre* or *en l'air,* in any given direction.

DÉGAGÉ EN TOURNANT (day-gah-zhay ahn toor-NAHn). Literally, disengaged turning. A rotation of the working leg on the axis of the hip joint, performed *à terre* or *en l'air* (Cecchetti method). For example, from the pose *arabesque en croisé,* the dancer turns toward the raised leg, rotating the body in the hip joint to finish in the pose *croisé devant.* Also called *détourné d'adage* when performed slowly.

DÉGAGER (day-gah-zHAY). Literally, to disengage. To free the foot in preparation for the execution of a step.

DEHORS, EN (ahn dih-OHR). Literally, outward. 1. A term used to indicate that a movement originates in the front

40

and circles toward the back, for example, *rond de jambe en dehors.* 2. A term used to indicate that in a *pirouette* the turn is made toward the working or raised foot; that is, if the turn is made on the right foot it will be to the left. 3. A term used to indicate the turned-out position of the legs and feet from the hip joints.

DEMI (d'mee). Half.

DEMI-BRAS (d'mee-BRAH). Literally, half arms or arms at the halfway position. See *Bras, demi.*

DEMI-CONTRETEMPS (d'mee-kohn-treh-TAHn). Literally, half counter beat. 1. A compound step consisting of a *coupé dessus* on the *demi-pointe, tombé.* 2. In the Cecchetti method, the *demi-contretemps* consists of *temps levé, chassé croisé en avant.*

DEMI-DÉTOURNÉ (d'mee-day-toor-NAY). Literally, half turned aside. A half turn on both feet, turning toward the back foot. The feet change so that the back foot becomes the front foot when the turn is completed. If the dancer starts facing the audience, he will finish with his back to the audience.

DEMI-HAUTEUR (d'mee-oh-TUHR). Literally, half-height. A position of the foot at midheight. The leg is considered at full height, or 90°, when it extends in the air at hip level. *Demi-hauteur* is a position of the leg at 45°, or midway between the ground and hip level. Also called *demi-position.*

Demi-hauteur

41

DEMI-PLIÉ (d'mee-plee-AY).
Literally, half-bent. A half
bending of the knees. The
knees are bent only as far as
is possible while still keeping the heels securely placed
on the floor. The *demi-plié*
underlies practically all the
movements of ballet, and it
is impossible to be a good
ballet dancer if one does not
have a good *demi-plié*. See also *Plié*.

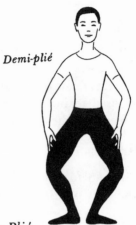

Demi-plié

DEMI-POINTES, SUR LES (siur lay d'mee-PWAHnt). Literally, on the half points. Indicates that the dancer stands on
the balls of the feet. The singular, *la demi-pointe*, is also
used. See *Pied à quart, Pied à demi, Pied à trois-quarts*.

DEMI-POSITION (d'mee-poh-zee-syon). Literally, half position. See *Demi-hauteur*.

DEMI-ROND DE JAMBE (d'mee-rohn dih ZHAHnB). Literally, half circle of the leg. See *Rond de jambe*.

Demi-rond de jambe à terre (d'mee-rohn dih zhahnb ah
TAIR). Literally, half circle of the leg on the ground. It may
be performed *en dehors* or *en dedans*. The working foot is
extended *pointe tendue* either to the fourth position front
(for *en dehors*) or to the fourth position back (for *en dedans*); the toes describe an arc on the floor, finishing in the
second position.

DEMI-SECONDE POSITION (d'mee-seh-gohnd poh-zee-
syon). Literally, half-second position. A position of the
arms midway between first and second positions. See *Bras,
positions de*.

DEMI-TOUR (d'mee-TOOR). Literally, half turn.

DÉROULÉ (day-roo-LAY). Unwound; unwinding.

42

DERRIÈRE (dih-ree-AIR). Behind; back. For example, *à la quatrième derrière*.

DESCENDANT, EN (ahn dih-sahn-DAHn). Literally, coming down. A term used to indicate that the dancer advances from the back of the stage to the front.

DESSOUS (dih-soo). Literally, under. A term used to indicate that the working foot passes in back of the supporting foot. For example, *coupé dessous, assemblé dessous.*

DESSUS (dih-siu). Literally, over. A term used to indicate that the working foot passes in front of the supporting foot. For example, *coupé dessus, assemblé dessus.*

DÉTIRÉ, TEMPS (tahn day-tih-RAY). Literally, time drawn out, or drawing-out movement. A stretching exercise in which the dancer holds the heel of the working foot in the corresponding hand, stretches the leg forward, and carries it to the second position *en l'air.*

DÉTOURNÉ (day-toor-NAY). Literally, turned, or turning aside in a direction contrary to normal. A pivot turn of the body on both feet (*demi-pointe* or *pointe*), turning toward the back foot and making a complete turn. The feet change during the turn so that the back foot finishes in front. See also *Demi-détourné.*

Détourné d'adage (day-toor-nay dah-DAZH). Literally, turning aside of *adage*. A rotation of the body from an *arabesque* position to the second position or fourth position front (French school). See *Dégagé en tournant.*

DEUX (duh). Two.

DEUXIÈME (duh-zYEM). Second.

DEVANT (dih-VAHn). In front. For example, *à la quatrième devant.*

43

DÉVELOPPÉ, TEMPS (tahn day-vloh-PAY). Literally, time developed, or developing movement. The generic term for the unfolding movement of the foot in an extension of the leg. *Développés* may be performed in any given direction and into any given pose, on the whole foot, the *demi-pointe*, full *pointe*, or *en fondu*. For example, *développé à la seconde*.

Développé en fondu (day-vloh-pay ahn fohn-DIU). A developing movement of one foot made while the supporting knee bends in *demi-plié*.

Développé passé (day-vloh-pay pah-SAY). Literally, developed movement passing. The foot passes from front to back (*développé passé en arrière*), or back to front (*développé passé en avant*), with a developing movement. It may be performed *en l'air, piqué, relevé*, or *sauté*.

DIAGHILEV, SERGEI (syair-GAY-ee DYAH-gih-lev), 1872–1929. He was born in Perm, Russia, a member of the Russian nobility. Although educated for the law, his interests lay in the arts and the artistic life of St. Petersburg where he went in 1890. He joined a circle of young painters and musicians and together they founded in 1899 the magazine *Mir Isskoustva (The World of Art)* which became a strong influence on the development of the arts in Russia. Also in 1899 he was appointed to the staff of the Imperial Theaters. He supervised the productions of several highly successful operas and ballets. Between the years 1904 and 1908 Diaghilev staged successful art exhibitions in St. Petersburg and brought Russian art to Paris with considerable success. In 1908 he presented the famous Russian basso, Feodor Chaliapin, in the title role of *Boris Godunov* at the Paris Opéra. In 1909 he presented a season of Russian Ballet at the Théâtre Châtelet in Paris. With Michel Fokine as choreographer and a roster of great Russian dancers from the Imperial Ballet, including Anna Pavlova, Tamara Karsavina, Vaslav Nijinsky, Adolph Bolm, and Mikhail Mordkin, all of whom became world famous, the Russian Ballet scored such a triumph in Paris that reverberations were heard around the world. In 1910 Diaghilev again produced a season of Russian Ballet in Paris, this time at the Opéra. In 1911 he decided to establish his company as a permanent organization in the Western world. Up to that time all of the dancers had been members of the Imperial Ballet and engagements were limited to the summer months when they were on vacation. From 1911 to 1929 the Diaghilev Ballet Russe was among the chief artistic attractions of all of the great European capitals. In 1913 and 1917 they toured South America, in 1916 and 1917 the United States. Although Diaghilev was not a musician, a dancer, or a painter, he had an extraordinary ability to bring together artists of talent and to supervise their collaboration in producing great balletic works of art.

DIAGONALE, EN (ahn dya-goh-NAHL). Literally, in diagonal. A term used to indicate that a step is to be performed traveling diagonally across the stage. For example, *chaînes tours en diagonale.*

DIDELOT, CHARLES LUDWIG (sharl LUHD-veeg DEE-d'loh), 1767–1837. Born in Stockholm. His father was a French dancer and choreographer, his mother Swedish. He studied first under his father, later with Dauberval, then August Vestris. He worked with Noverre and assimilated his artistic ideas. Didelot introduced many changes in stage costuming. He is credited with introducing flesh-colored tights for women. He is also the inventor of the use of the wire for "flying"—a device widely used in ballet productions during the Romantic period when sylphs and wilis soared in the air. He was the choreographer of *Flora and*

Zephyr and many other celebrated ballets. He is highly revered in Russia as one of the chief architects of their ballet. See *Russian school.*

DIRECTIONS OF THE BODY. The turning of the body to various directions in space in order that the dancer may present various views of his body (profile, three-quarter, full face, back) to the audience, thus giving more color and variety to his movements. Directions in space include *de face, en croisé (devant* and *derrière), en écarté (devant* and *derrière), en effacé (devant* and *derrière), en épaulé (devant* and *derrière), de côté,* and *dos au public.* See also *Positions of the body,* and frontispiece diagram.

DIVERTISSEMENT (dih-vair-tees-MAHn). Literally, diversion. 1. A dance, complete in itself, executed by one or more persons. 2. A suite of dances called *entrées,* each complete in itself, inserted into a full-length classical ballet to display the talents of various members of the company. 3. A dance interlude in an opera.

DOS À DOS (doh-za-DOH). Back to back.

DOS AU PUBLIC (doh-zoh piu-BLEEK). With one's back to the public, or audience.

DOUBLE (DOO-blih). Double. For example, *battement frappé double.*

DOUBLÉ (doo-BLAY). Doubled. For example, *sissonne doublée.*

DROITE, À (ah DRWAHT). To the right.

Dos au public

46

Écarté derrière   *Écarté devant*

ℰ

ÉCARTÉ (ay-kar-TAY). Literally, separated; thrown wide apart. 1. A direction of the body in space in which the dancer presents a three-quarter view of his body, standing or moving at an oblique angle to the audience, with the legs in the second position. *Derrière:* extend leg to upper corner of stage. *Devant:* extend leg to lower corner of stage. See *Directions of the body, Positions of the body,* and frontispiece diagram. 2. A form of *grands changements* in which the legs are thrown to the second position as the dancer springs high into the air.

ÉCHAPPÉ, TEMPS (tahn-zay-shah-PAY). Literally, time escaped or slipped; escaping movement. *Échappé* may be performed with a *sauté* or a *relevé.* The legs escape from the fifth position to the second or fourth position.

Échappé battu (ay-shah-pay bah-TIU). Literally, escaping movement beaten. An *échappé sauté à la seconde* performed with a beating together of the calves of the legs on the return to the fifth position.

Échappé changé (ay-shah-pay shahn-ZHAY). Literally, escaping movement changing. An *échappé à la seconde,* either *sauté* or *relevé,* with a change of feet on the close in the fifth position.

47

Échappé royale (ay-shah-pay rwah-YAL). Literally, a beaten *échappé*, with the beat taking place before the legs open to the second position.

Échappé sans changer (ay-shah-pay sahn shahn-ZHAY). Literally, escaping movement without changing. An *échappé à la seconde,* either *sauté* or *relevé,* without a change of feet on the close in the fifth position.

Échappé sauté (ay-shah-pay soh-TAY). Literally, escaping movement, jumping. From the fifth position, spring into the air and alight in the second or fourth position, in a *demi-plié.* Spring into the air again and return to the fifth position *demi-plié,* with or without a change of feet. *Échappé sauté* may be performed *grand* or *petit.*

Échappé sauté, grand (grahn-day-shah-pay soh-TAY). Literally, big escaping movement, jumping. Spring upward, keeping both legs tightly crossed over each other in the fifth position *en l'air* until the maximum height of the jump has been reached. Then allow the legs to escape to the second or fourth position. Finish *fondu* in the open position on the floor. To close reverse all the movements.

Échappé sauté, petit (p'tee-tay-shah-pay soh-TAY). Literally, small escaping movement, jumping. Open the legs to the second or fourth position *en l'air* while making a small jump and alight in a *demi-plié* in the second or fourth position. Then return to the fifth position with a *sauté,* with or without a change of feet.

Échappé sur les pointes (ay-shah-pay siur lay PWAHnt). Literally, escaping movement on the points. From the fifth position the legs open with a *relevé* to the second or fourth position on the *pointes* or *demi-pointes,* with or without a change of feet.

ÉCOLE (ay-KOHL). School; i.e., *école français, école russe.*

48

EFFACÉ (eh-fah-SAY), **EFFACÉE** (eh-fah-SAY). Literally, shaded. A direction of the body in space in which the dancer presents a three-quarter view of his body standing or moving at an oblique angle to the audience with the legs in the fourth position, the leg farthest from the audience being the front leg. See *Directions of the body* and *Positions of the body*.

Effacé derrière (eh-fah-say dih-ree-AIR). Literally, shaded in back. Face in an *effacé* direction, with the back foot (foot nearest the audience) pointing to the fourth position either *pointe tendue à terre* or *en l'air*. See *Positions of the body* and frontispiece diagram.

Effacé derrière　　　　　　　　　　*Effacé devant*

Effacé devant (eh-fah-say dih-VAHn). Literally, shaded in front. Face in an *effacé* direction, with the front foot (foot farthest from the audience) pointing to the fourth position either *pointe tendue à terre* or *en l'air*. See *Positions of the body* and frontispiece diagram.

Effacé en arrière (eh-fah-say ahn-nah-ree-AIR). Literally, shaded moving backward. The direction in which a given step is executed. Also called *ouvert en arrière*. See *Directions of the body*.

49

Effacé en avant (eh-fah-say ahn-nah-VAHn). Literally, shaded moving forward. The direction in which a given step is executed. Also called *ouvert en avant*. See *Directions of the body*.

ÉLANCÉ (ay-lahn-SAY). Literally, darted; darting. A term used to indicate that a step is to be made in a darting manner, as in *assemblé élancé*.

ÉLANCER (ay-lahn-SAY). To dart.

ÉLÉVATION (ay-lay-vah-SYOn). Literally, elevation. A term used to indicate the height of the jump attained by a dancer. There are steps of *grande élévation,* such as *grands jetés, grands changements,* etc., in which the dancer exerts all his strength to rise as high from the floor as possible. There are also steps involving a springing action, or *ballon,* such as *jetés, assemblés, coupés, cabrioles,* etc., in which the dancer bounds lightly.

ÉLÉVATION, TEMPS D' (tahn day-lay-vah-SYOn). Literally, time or beats of *élévation;* that is, raised or lifted movements. The generic term applied to all steps that involve a spring or jump into the air as opposed to *terre à terre* steps, which stay close to the floor. Also called *pas d'élévation*.

EMBOÎTÉ, PAS (pah-zahn-bwah-TAY). Literally, boxed-in step. A type of *jeté* performed without a brush of the working foot. The dancer springs from one foot to the other, finishing with the raised leg in a low *attitude* position. *Emboîté* may be performed *devant* or *derrière*. Also called *petit jeté* and *jeté passé*.

Emboîté en tournant (ahn-bwah-tay ahn toor-NAHn). Literally, boxed-in turning. A series of *emboîtés devant* performed with a half turn of the body on each *emboîté*.

Emboîté sur les pointes (ahn-bwah-tay siur lay PWAHnT).

Literally, boxed in on the toes. A step from the technique of dancing on the toes. From the fifth position on *pointes* or *demi-pointes*, open the back foot to the second position and bring forward in a circular movement to close to a tight fifth position *en pointe* in front of the supporting foot, remaining on the *pointes* or *demi-pointes*. The reverse of this movement is called *déboîté* or *emboîté en reculant*.

ENCHAÎNEMENT (ahn-shain-MAHn). Literally, linking. A series of given steps performed to a musical phrase or phrases. In English, it is called *combination*.

ENLÈVEMENT (ahn-lehv-MAHn). Literally, carrying or lifting. The lifting of the ballerina by her cavalier or partner.

ENSEMBLE (ahn-SAHn-blih). Literally, whole. 1. A group of dancers; the *corps de ballet*. 2. Together.

ENTRECHAT (ahn-trih-SHAH). Literally, interweaving. Derived from the Italian *intreccaire*, to interweave or braid. A step of elevation in which the dancer crosses his legs in the air, beating the calves against each other and changing the feet. The noun *entrechat* is qualified by the ordinals *trois, quatre, cinq, six, sept, huit, dix,* according to the number of crossings made. Even numbers finish on both feet in *demi-plié,* odd numbers on one foot in *demi-plié.*

Entrechat cinq (ahn-trih-shah SANK). Five crossings, two changes of foot. The *entrechat cinq* may be performed *derrière* or *devant*. The beating of the legs is the same as for *entrechat quatre* but the finish of the step is on one foot, as in *entrechat trois*. To perform the *entrechat cinq derrière,* spring into the air from the fifth position, open the legs to a small second position in the air, cross the legs in the air, beating the calf of the leg that was in front behind the calf of the other leg, open the legs again to a small

51

second position in the air, and, changing, descend into *fondu* on the front foot with the back foot pointed *sur le cou-de-pied derrière.* To perform the *entrechat cinq devant,* finish with the front foot pointed *sur le cou-de-pied devant.*

Entrechat cinq fermé (ahn-trih-shah sank fair-MAY). From the second position, spring into the air, cross the feet in the fifth position in the air, open to a small second position in the air, cross the legs again in the air with a change of feet in the fifth position, open to a small second position and descend into the fifth position *fondu,* with a change of feet. Also called *royale double fermé.*

Entrechat cinq ouvert (ahn-trih-shah sank OO-VAIR). Spring into the air from the beginning fifth position, open the legs to a small second position in the air, cross the front foot behind the back foot in the air, open to a small second position in the air, cross the legs again in the air with a change of feet, open to a wide second position, and descend into the second position *fondu.* Also called *royale double ouvert.*

Entrechat cinq ramassé (ahn-trih-shah sank rah-mah-SAY). See *Sissonne fermée battue.*

Entrechat dix (ahn-trih-shah DEES). Ten crossings, five changes of feet. This is the greatest number of crossings known to have been made on one jump by male dancers of an exceptionally high elevation or jump.

Entrechat huit (ahn-trih-shah WHEET). Eight crossings, four changes of feet. The *entrechat huit* may be thought of as a double *entrechat quatre* with the descent into the fifth position *fondu* coming after the second *quatre.*

Entrechat quatre (ahn-trih-shah KAH-trih). Four crossings, two changes of feet; open, beat, open, close to the fifth position. To perform the *entrechat quatre,* spring into the air from the fifth position, open the legs to a small second position in the air, cross the legs in the air, beating the calf of the leg that was front behind the calf of the other leg, open the legs again to a small second position in the air, and descend into the fifth position *fondu,* with the feet in the starting position.

Entrechat sept (ahn-trih-shah SET). Seven crossings, three changes of feet. The *entrechat sept,* like the *entrechat trois* and the *entrechat cinq,* finishes on one foot with the other foot pointed *sur le cou-de-pied derrière* or *devant;* or, it may also finish extended in the air to the second position or raised to *attitude.* To perform the *entrechat sept,* make an *entrechat six* and instead of finishing in the fifth position descend *fondu* on one foot.

Entrechat six (ahn-trih-shah SEES). Six crossings, three changes of foot; open, beat, open, beat, open, close to the fifth position. To perform the *entrechat six,* spring into the air from the beginning fifth position, open the legs to a small second position in the air, cross the front foot behind the other foot, open to a small second position in the air, cross the legs again changing feet, open to a small second position in the air, descend into the fifth position *fondu* with another change of feet. (If the step begins with the right foot in front, it will finish with the right foot in back.)

Entrechat trois (ahn-trih-shah TRWAH). Three crossings with one change of feet; beat, open, change feet. *Entrechat trois* may be performed *derrière* or *devant.* To perform *entrechat trois derrière,* spring into the air from the fifth position, beating the calves of the legs against each other. Open the legs to the second position in the air, and descend into a *fondu* on the foot that was behind, with the other foot pointed *sur le cou-de-pied derrière.* To perform the *entrechat trois devant,* bring the back foot to a point *sur le cou-de-pied devant* after the beat and open to the second position.

53

ENTRECHAT DE VOLÉE (ahn-trih-shah dih voh-LAY). Literally, interweaving flying.

Entrechat six de volée (ahn-trih-shah sees dih voh-LAY). After a preparatory step, such as *glissade derrière* or a *failli,* the dancer performs an *assemblé dessus porté* with six crossings of the legs, three changes of feet: open, beat, open, beat, open, close to the fifth position *fondu.* A term of the Russian and Cecchetti schools. Also called *entrechat cinq de volée* (French school).

ENTRÉE (ahn-TRAY). Literally, entrance; entry. 1. A *divertissement* executed by a group of dancers. The *ballets de la cour,* or court ballets, of the seventeenth and eighteenth centuries were composed of a number of acts—generally five. Each act consisted of a number of *entrées,* or dances, by one or more groups of dancers who, by their movements, expressed part of the theme of the ballet. 2. The beginning of a *grand pas de deux* in which the ballerina and the *premier danseur* make their entrance.

ENTRELACÉ (ahn-trih-lah-SAY). Literally, interlaced. For example, *jeté entrelacé.*

ENVELOPÉE (ahn-vloh-PAY). Literally, enveloped. A movement in which the working leg executes a *grand rond de jambe en dedans* and whips into a *cou-de-pied* or *raccourci* position while the body is turning *en dedans relevé* or *sauté* (French school).

ÉPAULÉ (ay-poh-LAY), **ÉPAU-LÉE** (ay-poh-LAY). Literally, shouldered. A position of the body in which the dancer presents a three-quarter view of the body,

Épaulé

standing or moving at an oblique angle to the audience, with the arm and shoulder nearest the audience extended forward and the corresponding leg extended in an *arabesque*. See *Positions of the body* and frontispiece diagram.

ÉPAULEMENT (ay-pohl-MAH*n*). Literally, shouldering. The generic term for the use of the upper body or shoulders in ballet movement. *Épaulement* invests movement with style and artistry, providing color that would otherwise be lacking if all movements were performed directly facing the audience.

ÉQUILIBRE (ay-kee-LEE-brih). Literally, equilibrium; aplomb. The balancing of the body over the legs and feet.

ÉTENDRE (ay-TAH*n*-drih). To stretch.

ÉTOILE (ay-TWAHL). Literally, star. The principal dancer of a company: the French term for the Italian *prima ballerina*.

EXERCICES À LA BARRE (egz-ehr-sees ah lah BAHR). Literally, exercises at the bar. The generic term for the group of special exercises performed daily, at the *barre*, by all ballet dancers: see also *Barre*. The study of academic classical ballet technique begins with the simplest forms of these exercises at the *barre: demi-pliés; grands-pliés; battements tendus, dégagés, fondus,* and *frappés; ronds de jambe, à terre* and *en l'air; développés; grands battements;* and the like. While these exercises, as a whole, have as their purpose the development of strength in feet, thighs, and back, the gaining of aplomb or balance, the turning of the legs *en dehors* (outward) from the hip joints, and the freeing and lightening of the limbs so that they will move quickly and lightly, each individual exercise has its own function. The *plié,* for example, develops the elasticity of the muscles around the knee and stretches the ligaments and tendons of the hip to make possible the 180° turnout of the thighs and feet. As the dancer progresses in his training the exercises at the *barre* become more complex. They are performed daily as warming-up movements for the ballet class and always precede performance on the stage.

EXERCICES AU MILIEU (egz-ehr-sees oh mee-LYIU). Literally, exercises in the center. The generic term for the special exercises similar to the *exercices à la barre* but performed in the center of the practice room without the support of the *barre*. The purpose of these exercises is to further the development of balance, strength, and co-ordination and to increase agility. Also called *center practice*.

EXTENSION (egz-tahn-SYON). The act of extending the legs into space. A dancer is said to have a good *extension* when able to hold the leg at a 135° angle.

Extension

De face

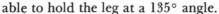

FACE, DE (dih FAHS). Literally, facing. A direction of the body in space, facing straight front to the audience. See frontispiece diagram.

FACE, EN (ahn FAHS). Opposite.

FAILLI, PAS (pah fi-YEE). Literally, giving-way step. From the fifth position, facing *en croisé*, spring into the air, turning to *effacé* direction, descend on the front foot *en fondu* with the back leg extended in the air, immediately make a *chassé* through the first position (*demi-plié*), and finish in the fourth position with the weight on the front foot, front knee bent in *demi-plié*.

FERMÉ (fair-MAY), **FERMÉE** (fair-MAY). Literally, closed. A term used to indicate that both feet are in a closed position, such as the fifth position, or that the feet are brought into the fifth position at the end of the step. For example, *jeté fermé, sissonne fermée*.

FIGURE (fih-GIUR). Literally, figure; form; shape. The pattern described by a dancer in performing a set of steps.

FILER (fee-LAY). To spin. For example, *filer une pirouette*.

FLÉCHIR (flay-SHEER). To bend.

FLIC-FLAC (flihk-flahk). A compound step composed of three whipping, or lashing, movements of the leg (Russian school). From a second position *en l'air*, whip one foot downward, brushing the toes against the floor and bending the knee so that the arched foot finishes in front of the supporting ankle; then throw the foot outward to the second position without brushing the floor, and again whip in, brushing the toes against the floor and finishing arched behind the ankle. This movement may be reversed (brush back, brush front). Also called *petits fouettés* (Cecchetti method).

Flic-flac en tournant (flihk-flahk ahn toor-NAHn). A compound step consisting of two whipping movements of the working leg (*petits fouettés*) while turning on the supporting foot. For a *flic-flac en tournant en dedans*, from the

57

second position *en l'air,* sweep the working foot forcefully downward and across the front of the supporting foot to a *croisé* position; then bend the knee and strike the toes forcefully against the floor behind the supporting foot, while the supporting foot makes a *relevé* and a complete turn; finish with a *fondu* on the supporting leg, with the working foot pointed *sur le cou-de-pied derrière.* For a *flic-flac en tournant en dehors,* reverse the movements.

FOKINE, MICHEL (mih-SHEL FOH-keen), 1880–1942. Dancer and choreographer born in Russia. He was called the twentieth-century Noverre. Fokine brought great reforms to ballet. He fused the arts of pantomime and dance, making the dance itself express the dramatic line of the action or story. He revitalized the art of ballet, bringing to it a flow of movement and plasticity in place of static, pedantic technical display. A great choreographer, Fokine demanded an organic fusion of inspirational music, dance, and painting, together with a unified construction and expression. He was the first choreographer to be associated with the Ballet Russe de Sergei Diaghilev. A member of the original group of artists who founded and formed this company, he created its original historical repertoire.

FONDU (fohn-DIU), **FONDUE** (fohn-DIU). Literally, sinking down; melting. 1. The descent from a jump or from a *relevé* into a *plié,* when the use of the instep, or insteps, is co-ordinated with the bend of the knee or knees. 2. A lowering of the body made by bending the knee of the supporting leg, as in *arabesque fondue* or *développé fondu.* 3. The finish of a step when the dancer alights on one foot with a co-ordinated rolling down through the instep and bending of the knee, then carefully places the other foot in the fifth position, ending in a *demi-plié* on both feet. For example, *sissonne fondue.*

FOUETTÉ (fweh-TAY). Literally, whipped. A whipping movement. The term is applied both to movements of the body and to movements of the legs.

Fouetté, demi (d'mee fweh-TAY). Literally, whipped half movement. This is a form of *fouetté en l'air,* in which the dancer makes one quarter turn in the air instead of a half turn. Stand facing the audience, with one leg extended to the second position *en l'air.* With a sharp movement, turn the body in profile to the audience, while the leg rotates in the hip socket; the finishing pose is *arabesque.* This step may be performed *en relevé, piqué,* or *sauté.*

Fouetté en l'air (fweh-tay ahn LAIR). Literally, whipped movement in the air. The dancer makes a half turn with the body while the supporting leg turns in place, the movement being a rotation in the hip socket. The position changes from *grand quatrième devant* to *arabesque.* May be performed *relevé, piqué* or *sauté.*

Fouetté en tournant, petit (p'tee fweh-tay ahn toor-NAHn). Literally, small whipped movement turning. See *Flic-flac en tournant.*

Fouetté, grand (grahn fweh-TAY). Literally, large whipped movement. This is a form of *fouetté en l'air* in which the performer makes a whole turn in the air instead of a half turn. 1. Stand in *arabesque fondue ouverte,* carry the working leg forcefully downward, striking the toes against the floor, at the same time make a *relevé* on the supporting foot, and immediately lift the working leg to the fourth position front (profile to audience), execute a half turn on the supporting foot (*demi-pointe*) with the working leg remaining extended forward; sharply twist (rotate) to *arabesque,* finishing in the starting position. This step may also be performed *sauté.* 2. Face the audience, with the leg extended to the second position *en l'air,* carry the working leg forcefully downward, striking the toes against the floor, at the same time bend the supporting knee in a *plié;* immediately, lift the working leg to the fourth position front with a *relevé* or a *sauté,* while the body turns to the upper corner of the stage, and with a sharp twist in the air turn (rotate) to *arabesque croisée,* finishing *en fondu.* Also called *grand fouetté en tournant.*

Fouetté, petit (p'tee fweh-TAY). Literally, small whipped movement. This is a whipped movement of the leg. From a second position *en l'air,* a few inches above the floor, sharply sweep the toes of the working foot down and across, either in front of, or in back of, the supporting foot, finishing with the working knee bent and the foot pointed *sur le cou-de-pied, devant,* or *derrière.*

Fouetté raccourci (fweh-tay rah-koor-SEE). Literally, whipped movement shortened. A movement similar to the *petit fouetté.* From the second position *en l'air,* the working foot is cut sharply behind the supporting leg, the action being made by bending the working knee without lowering the thigh.

Fouetté rond de jambe en tournant (fweh-tay rohn dih zhahnb ahn toor-NAHn). Literally, whipped circle of the leg turning. A form of *grande pirouette* in which the dancer makes a complete turn on one foot while the other executes a *demi-grand rond de jambe en dehors* and a *battement* at the knee. These are usually performed in a series. They may be executed turning *en dehors* or *en dedans.*

FRAPPÉ (frah-PAY). Striking, as in *battement frappé.*

FRENCH SCHOOL. Ballet, as we know it today, originated in France where Louis XIV (himself an accomplished ballet dancer) founded the Royal Academy of Dancing in 1661. Pierre Beauchamp, Ballet Master to the King, codified the steps and movements in use in that day and set the rules, including the five positions of the feet, which still govern ballet today. Jean Georges Noverre, the great eighteenth-century ballet master and reformer, brought in the use of anatomical principles in technical training. The French school has always stressed charm and elegance, however, rather than technical virtuosity. The influence of the French school spread throughout Europe and underlies all balletic training.

G

GARGOUILLADE (gahr-gee-AHD). Literally, dabbling or paddling. Dabbling movement. The *gargouillade* resembles a *pas de chat* with quick *ronds de jambe en l'air*. For a *gargouillade en dehors,* from the fifth position, execute a double *rond de jambe en l'air en dehors* with the front foot; spring onto that foot while executing a double *rond de jambe en l'air en dedans* with the other foot; close in the fifth position front *fondu.* For a *gargouillade en dedans,* from the fifth position, execute a double *rond de jambe en l'air en dedans* with the back foot; spring onto that foot while executing a double *rond de jambe en l'air en dehors* with the other foot; close in the fifth position front *fondu.* For a *gargouillade volée,* from the fifth position, or from *pointe tendue derrière,* execute a single or double *rond de jambe en l'air en dedans,* finishing *raccourci* (working foot pointing at supporting knee); spring into the air, changing feet; *développé* the other foot to *effacé devant à terre* or *en l'air.*

GAUCHE, À (ah GOHSH). To the left.

GENOU (zhnoo). Knee.

GLISSADE (glee-SAHD). Derived from *glisser,* to glide. Gliding step. *Glissade* is a *terre à terre* step, a linking movement between steps of high elevation. It usually precedes high springing or leaping steps, providing the impetus for the elevation. From a *demi-plié* in the fifth position, extend one leg and glide it on the floor to a strongly arched or pointed position a few inches above the floor; with a small spring from the supporting foot, shift the weight to the pointing foot with a *fondu* movement so that the positions of the legs are now reversed. Then draw the pointing foot into the fifth position *demi-plié. Glissades* may be performed with a change of feet, *changée (dessous* or *dessus);* without a change of feet, *derrière* and *devant; en arrière, en avant,* and *sur les pointes.*

Glissade changée (glee-sahd shahn-ZHAY). Literally, gliding changing feet. The foot initiating the action is extended to the second position, and the closing to the fifth position will involve a change of feet; that is, if the right foot is front in the fifth position and the *glissade* is made to the right, the finish of the step will find the left foot front in fifth position. The Cecchetti method has specified names for the *glissade changée dessous* and the *glissade changée dessus.* If the right foot is front at the start of the *glissade* (traveling to the right) and finishes in the back, the movement is called *glissade dessous.* If the right foot is back at the start of the *glissade* (traveling to the right) and finishes in the front, it is called *glissade dessus. Glissade changée* travels to the side.

Glissade derrière (glee-sahd dih-ree-AIR). Literally, gliding in back. The back foot initiates the action with a gliding movement to the second position. The front foot makes the closing to the fifth position in front. The *glissade derrière* does not have a change of feet; the step travels to the side.

Glissade devant (glee-sahd dih-VAHn). Literally, gliding in front. The front foot initiates the action with a gliding movement to the second position. The back foot makes the closing to the fifth position in back. The *glissade devant* does not have a change of feet; the step travels to the side.

Glissade en arrière (glee-sahd ah*n*-nah-ree-AIR). Literally, gliding backward. The back foot initiates the action with a gliding movement to the fourth position back; the step travels to the back.

Glissade en avant (glee-sahd ah*n*-nah-VAH*n*). Literally, gliding forward. The front foot initiates the action with a gliding movement to the fourth position front; the step travels to the front.

Glissade précipitée (glee-sahd pray-sip-ih-TAY). Literally, accelerated gliding step. An extremely quick and small form of *glissade* performed between musical beats as a preparation for a step, as a *piqué* in *arabesque*.

Glissade sur les pointes (glee-sahd siur lay PWAH*n*T). Literally, gliding on the toes. The initial step is made on *pointes*, the closing to the fifth position on *pointes* and *fondu* in fifth position. It may be performed in any given direction.

GLISSÉ (glee-SAY). Literally, glided or gliding. A term used to indicate that a step or movement is performed gliding on the floor, as in *pas de basque glissé; battements glissés.*

GLISSER (glee-SAY). To glide.

GRAND (grah*n*), **GRANDE** (grah*n*d). Big; large; wide; deep.

H

HAUT, EN (ah*n*-NOH). High. A term used to indicate a high position of the arms or legs.

HAUTEUR (oh-TUHR). Height. The leg is said to be *à la hauteur* when it is raised at a 90°, or right angle to the hip.

ℐ

INCLINÉ (an-klee-NAY), **INCLINÉE** (an-klee-NAY). Inclined. For example, *tête inclinée de côté,* head inclined sideways.

ITALIAN SCHOOL. It was founded by Carlo Blasis, an Italian who had studied under French masters. Blasis recodified all that was known of ballet technique to his day (1803–1878). A student of anatomy, he extended the use of anatomical principles in developing the body into a dance instrument, making possible the achievement of greater technical dexterity. In so doing, he brought the Italian school to great virtuosity. He designed the format of the ballet class which is still used today in ballet training all over the world. The school reached its peak in Enrico Cecchetti, a pupil of Giovanni Lepri who had been a student of Blasis.

ℐ

JAMBE (zhahn*b*). Leg.

JETÉ, PAS (pah zheh-TAY). Literally, step thrown, or throwing step. A jump from one foot to the other, performed with a throwing movement of the leg. There are *jetés* of many types.

Jeté bateau (zheh-tay bah-TOH). Literally, boatlike throwing step. See *Ballotté, pas.*

Jeté battu (zheh-tay bah-TIU). Literally, beaten throwing step. A step of *petite batterie,* it may be performed *dessus* or *dessous.* To perform *jeté battu dessus,* from the fifth position *demi-plié,* make a *dégagé à la seconde* with the back foot, gliding it along the ground until it arrives at a position *à la demi-hauteur;* spring off the supporting foot, beat

64

the calves of the legs together, with the working leg coming down to beat in back of the supporting leg, throw the legs open and alight *fondu* on the working foot, with the other foot *sur le cou-de-pied derrière*. To perform *jeté battu dessous,* reverse the movements, beginning with the front foot.

Jeté de côté (zheh-tay dih koh-TAY). Literally, throwing step to the side. From the fifth position *demi-plié,* make a *dégagé à la seconde* with the working leg, gliding it along the floor until it reaches a position of 45° (or 90° if it is to be a *grand jeté*). Spring off the supporting foot, throwing it to the second position *en l'air,* travel to the side, alight *fondu* on the working foot, with the other foot pointing *sur le cou-de-pied devant* or *derrière* (or at the knee if it is a *grand jeté*). Also called *jeté fondu.*

Jeté dessous (zheh-tay dih-soo). Literally, throwing step, under. The *jeté* is said to be *dessous* when the front foot replaces the back foot at the finish of the step. From the fifth position *demi-plié,* make a *dégagé à la seconde* with the front foot, gliding it along the floor until it reaches a position *à la demi-hauteur.* Spring off the supporting foot, alight *fondu* on the working foot, slightly in back of and replacing the supporting foot, which is lifted and pointed *sur le cou-de-pied devant.*

This step is also called *jeté devant* and *jeté derrière,* as the result of a controversy as to whether the step takes its name from the foot that is raised at the end of the step or from the foot that is thrown at the beginning of the step. To avoid this controversy, the Syllabus Committee of the National Academy of Ballet has named the step *jeté dessous* because the action brings the working foot under the supporting foot on the change of weight.

Jeté dessus (zheh-tay dih-siu). Literally, throwing step, over. The *jeté* is said to be *dessus* when the back foot replaces the

65

front foot at the finish of the step. From the fifth position *demi-plié,* make a *dégagé à la seconde* with the back foot, gliding it along the floor until it reaches a position *à la demi-hauteur.* Spring off the supporting foot, alight *fondu* on the working foot slightly in front of and replacing the supporting foot, which is lifted and pointed *sur le cou-de-pied derrière.* Also called *jeté derrière* and *jeté devant.* See explanatory paragraph under *Jeté dessous.*

Jeté en arrière, grand (grah*n* zheh-tay ah*n*-nah-ree-AIR). Literally, large throwing step backward. From the fourth position *pointe tendue croisé devant,* transfer the weight by bringing the front foot backward, pressing the knee into a deep *demi-plié* (in *effacé* direction), at the same time stretching the other leg forward into a strongly pointed position slightly above the floor and leaning the body toward the working side with the arms in the fifth position front. Sweep the pointing foot backward with a strong thrust upward to 90°, at the same time leaping high into the air off the supporting foot. Alight in *attitude croisée devant en fondu.*

Jeté en arrière, petit (p'tee zheh-tay ah*n*-nah-ree-AIR). Literally, small throwing step forward. From the fifth position *demi-plié,* make a *dégagé à la quatrième derrière* with the back foot, gliding it along the floor until it reaches a position, *à la demi-hauteur.* Spring off the supporting foot and alight *fondu* on the working foot, with the other leg extended *à la quatrième devant en l'air* or *sur le cou-de-pied devant.* It may be performed *de face, en croisé,* or *en effacé.*

Jeté en attitude (zheh-tay ah*n*-nah-tee-TIUD). Literally, throwing step finishing in *attitude* position.

Jeté en avant, grand (grah*n* zheh-tay ah*n*-nah-VAH*n*). Literally, large throwing step forward. From the fourth position *pointe tendue croisé derrière,* transfer the weight by bringing the back foot forward and pressing the knee into a deep *demi-plié* (in *effacé* direction), at the same time stretching the other leg back into a strongly pointed position slightly above the floor and leaning the body toward the supporting side with the arms in the fifth position *en avant*. Sweep the pointing foot forward with a strong thrust upward to 90°, at the same time leaping high into the air off the supporting foot. Alight in *attitude* or *arabesque croisée en fondu*. It may also be performed starting *en effacé*, stepping *croisé*, and finishing in *attitude effacée* or in *épaulé*.

Jeté en avant, petit (p'tee zheh-tay ahn-nah-VAHn). Literally, small throwing step forward. From the fifth position *demi-plié*, make a *dégagé à la quatrième devant* with the front foot, gliding it along the floor until it reaches a position *à la demi-hauteur*. Spring off the supporting foot and alight *fondu* on the working foot, with the other leg extended *à la quatrième derrière en l'air* or *sur le cou-de-pied derrière*. It may be performed *de face, en croisé,* or *en effacé*.

Jeté en tournant (zheh-tay ahn toor-NAHn). Literally, throwing step turning. A composite step: *Tombé croisé devant, coupé dessous,* making a quarter turn *en dehors* and throwing the working leg to 90°, spring into the air continuing the turn, alight *fondu* on the working foot with the other leg raised in *attitude croisée derrière*. Repeat the *coupé* and the *jeté* as many times as desired. Also called *tour de reins* (French school).

Jeté en tournant entrelacé, grand (grahn zheh-tay ahn toor-nahn ahn-trih-lah-SAY). Literally, large throwing step turning interlaced. From a position *pointe tendue quatrième derrière,* turn sharply (rotate) toward the pointing foot, transferring the weight to it and executing a *grand* *battement devant* with the other foot; at the same time raise the arms through the fifth position *en avant* to the fifth position *en haut* and spring high into the air; turn the body sharply one half turn in the air, passing the legs with a scissorslike action so that the springing leg passes the working leg as the body arches in the air. Alight in *arabesque fondue* on the foot that made the *grand battement*. Also called *grand jeté en tournant, jeté entrelacé,* and *tour jeté. Tour jeté* is a grammatically incorrect corruption.

Jeté en tournant par demi-tours (zheh-tay ahn toor-nahn pahr d'mee-TOOR). Literally, throwing step turning by half turns. This is a term for a composite step consisting of a series of *jetés de côté,* traveling in a straight line and turning a half turn on each *jeté.* The body turns continuously in the same direction; that is, each half turn will be to the right, with the first *jeté* turning *en dedans* and the second *jeté* turning *en dehors.*

Jeté en tournant par terre (zheh-tay ahn toor-nahn pahr TAIR). Literally, throwing step turning close to the ground. A composite step consisting of a *jeté en avant en arabesque* low to the floor and traveling well forward, and a *coupé en tournant.*

Jeté entrelacé (zhey-tay ahn-trih-lah-SAY). Literally, throwing step interlaced. See *Jeté en tournant entrelacé, grand.*

Jeté enveloppé (zheh-tay ahn-vloh-PAY). Literally, throwing step enveloped. From the fifth position, brush the back foot to the second position *à la demi-hauteur* and execute to *demi-grand rond de jambe en dedans;* spring into the air, making a complete turn *en dedans;* alight on the working foot *en fondu,* with the other raised *en raccourci derrière* or *en attitude.* It may also be performed with a half turn.

Jeté fermé (zheh-tay fair-MAY). Literally, throwing step closed. A *jeté passé* finished by forcibly closing the raised foot into the fifth position *fondu.*

Jeté fermé de côté (zheh-tay fair-may dih koh-TAY). Literally, throwing step closed to the side. This step resembles the *glissade* except that it is performed with a high spring into the air instead of gliding along the floor. From the fifth position *demi-plié,* extend the working leg to the second position *en l'air* (45°), spring forcefully up into the air with the supporting foot, throwing it to second position *en l'air* (45°); traveling to the side of the first foot, alight on it in *fondu* with the second foot remaining in the second position *en l'air,* lower the second foot *pointe tendue à terre* and slide it into the fifth position *demi-plié.* This step may be performed *derrière, devant,* and *changé.* To make a *grand jeté fermé de côté,* throw the legs to 90°.

Jeté fouetté, grand (grahn zheh-tay fweh-TAY). Literally, large throwing step whipped. Execute a *grand jeté en avant;* at the height of the jump turn the body (rotating through the hips) toward the back leg, making a complete half turn in the air to face in the opposite direction; alight in *fondu* on the first foot with the other raised in front in *croisé* or *effacé* position.

Jeté, grand (grahn zheh-TAY). Literally, large throwing step. A *jeté* is said to be *grand* when the legs are raised at an angle of 90° with a correspondingly high leap.

Jeté passé (zheh-tay pah-SAY). Literally, throwing step passed. From a position *pointe tendue derrière,* step forward on the pointing foot, transferring the weight to a deep *demi-plié* and raising the other foot behind in a low *attitude* or *arabesque;* spring upward into the air off the supporting foot and alight, with a transference of weight in *attitude* or *arabesque fondue.* This step may also be reversed and performed *devant.* Also called *petit jeté, emboîté,* and *jeté en attitude.*

Jeté, petit (p'tee zheh-TAY). Literally, small throwing step. See *Emboîté* and *Jeté passé.*

Jeté renversé, grand (grahn zheh-tay rahn-vair-SAY). Literally, throwing step upset. Execute a *jeté volé de côté,* finishing with a *renversé* turn and *pas de bourée* with a back bend.

Jetés battements (zheh-tay baht-MAHn). Literally, throwing beating steps. These steps may be performed *dessus* or *dessous.* To perform *jetés battements dessus,* from the fifth position *demi-plié,* make a *dégagé à la seconde* with the back foot, gliding it along the ground until it arrives at a position *à la demi-hauteur;* spring off the supporting foot, alight *fondu* on the working foot, replacing the supporting foot, which is now lifted *sur le cou-de-pied derrière,* and immediately execute a *petit battement* to the *cou-de-pied devant,* finishing with a *dégagé à la seconde.* The *jeté* and *battement* may be repeated as many times as desired. To perform *jetés battements dessous,* reverse the movements, beginning with the front foot.

Jeté sur les pointes (zheh-tay siur lay PWAHnt). Literally, throwing step on the toes. 1. A quick *piqué* movement, transferring the weight from one point to the other in *pointe* work. 2. A transference of weight from a *demi-plié* to a *demi-pointe* or *pointe* position before lowering the heel of the supporting foot (Cecchetti method).

Jeté volé de côté (zheh-tay voh-lay dih koh-TAY). Literally, throwing step flying to the side. A *grand jeté de côté* finishing in *attitude croisée* or *arabesque croisée derrière.*

70

JOHANNSEN, CHRISTIAN (KRIS-tyahn yo-HAHN-sehn), 1817–1903. Swedish-born dancer and teacher. A pupil of Auguste Bournonville in Copenhagen, and chief teacher of the Imperial Ballet school in Russia from 1860 to 1903. See *Russian school.*

ℒ

LEÇON (leh-SOHN). Lesson.

LEOTARD (LEE-oh-tard). A tightly fitting one-piece garment covering the body from the neck to the thighs or to the ankles and sometimes covering the arms to the wrists, worn for ballet practice and on the stage.

LEPICQ, CHARLES FELIX REINHARDT AUGUST (sharl fay-LEEKS rine-hart oh-GOOST lih-PEEK), 1749–1806. Dancer, teacher, born in Alsace. A pupil of Noverre and leading dancer at the Paris Opéra during the reign of Louis XV. He later became one of the founding fathers of the Imperial Ballet in Russia, spending many years in St. Petersburg where he danced, taught, and choreographed. See *Russian school.*

LIGNE (LEEN-yih). Literally, line. The harmonious arrangement of the various parts of the body—head, shoulders, trunk, legs, and arms—in order to form beautiful and harmonious compositions of curves and straight lines in space. A good dancer displays a good outline of the body and thus pleases the eye of the spectator.

Ligne
The dancer forms lines (or designs) in space with the body.

LYRE, EN (ahn LEER). Literally, like a lyre. A modification of the fifth position *en haut* (or *en couronne*) of the arms, in which the arms resemble the shape of a lyre.

71

M

MAILLOT (mi-YOH). A tightly fitting garment covering the feet, legs, and body to the waist or armpits; tights.

MAIN (man). Hand.

MAÎTRE DE BALLET (meh-trih dih bah-LAY). Literally, master of ballet, or ballet master. Formerly, this term was applied to a choreographer and teacher. Today, the term is applied to the person in a ballet company who is responsible for rehearsing the ballets in the company repertoire and maintaining the standards of execution and performance.

MANÈGE, EN (ahn mah-NEZH). Literally, as at a riding school, or on a merry-go-round. A term used to indicate that a sequence of steps is to be performed in a circle around the stage.

MARQUER (mahr-KAY). 1. To stamp; to mark the accents in a step. 2. To "mark" or "walk through" an *enchaînement* or variation.

MÉTHODE (may-TOHD). Literally, method. There are various methods of teaching ballet. The three dominant schools of academic technique are the French, the Italian, and the Russian; the last named is actually a derivative of both the French and Italian. Within the framework of these basic schools there have been developed various systems of teaching laid down by great teachers. Thus, the Cecchetti method is a system of the Italian school; its principles were established during the mid-nineteenth century by Carlo Blasis and brought to their highest peak by Maestro Enrico Cecchetti during the early part of the twentieth century. The system taught at the Paris Opéra has its beginnings in the seventeeth and eighteenth centuries, based on the principles established by Pierre Beauchamp and Jean Georges

Noverre. The Imperial Ballet in Russia based its system of teaching on the French school instituted by Charles Didelot and later expounded by Christian Johannsen, a pupil of Bournonville who had been a pupil of Noverre. The Russian school also assimilated much of the Italian school from Cecchetti and other Italian dancers who appeared on the stages of the Imperial theaters. More recently, in Soviet Russia, the system of teaching has been that laid down by Agrippina Vaganova and based on the method taught at the Imperial school. In England there are two methods in favor, the Cecchetti, and the method of the Royal Academy of Dancing which stems from the French school. In the United States ballet is also in the process of forming its own national school, based on the elements of all three major schools. The National Academy of Ballet is pioneering in this work, having formulated its own graded syllabus, utilizing the virtuosity and brilliance of the Italian school, the grace, elegance, and charm of the French school, and the artistry and theatricality of the Russian school, all adapted to the American character and physique.

MILIEU, AU (oh-mee-LYIU). Literally, in the middle. A term used to indicate that certain exercises are performed in the center of the room, away from the *barre*. See *Exercices au milieu*.

MIMER (mee-MAY). Literally, to mime; to mimic; to ape. To express emotions or tell a story by means of gestures and facial expressions.

MONTER (mohn-TAY). Literally, to mount; to rise; *relever* or rise on the toes or the balls of the feet.

MOVEMENTS IN DANCING. There are seven types of movement in dancing: *élancer,* to dart; *étendre,* to stretch; *glisser,* to glide; *plier,* to bend; *relever,* to lift up; *sauter,* to leap; *tourner,* to turn.

𝒩

NOVERRE, JEAN GEORGES (zahn zhorzh noh-VEHR), 1727–1810. French ballet master who brought great reforms to the art of ballet. He fought for expressiveness in the dance at a time when dancers and ballet masters were content with performing steps merely for the sake of physical movement. Noverre declared the art of ballet to be imitative of life as acting is. He was responsible for many costume reforms as well. His *Letters on Dancing and Ballet,* first published in 1760 and republished many times since with translations into many languages, had enormous influence and improved ballet productions throughout Europe. See *French school.*

𝒪

OPPOSITION (ah-poh-zee-syon). The relationship of arm to leg where the arm position is in opposition to the working leg. Also refers to *épaulement* or relationship of the head and shoulders to the working leg when leg movements are *dessous.*

OUVERT (oo-vair), **OUVERTE** (oo-vairt). Opened; open. For example, *ouvert en avant; arabesque ouverte.*

OUVERTURE DE JAMBE (oo-vair-tiur dih zHAHnB). Literally, opening of the leg. See *Rond de jambe balancé.*

𝒫

PANTOMIMER (pahn-toh-mee-MAY). To pantomime. **See** *Mimer.*

PAR TERRE (pahr TAIR). On the ground.

PAS (pah). Literally, step. 1. A simple step in any direction. 2. A simple or compound movement that involves a transference of the weight of the body; for example, *pas jeté, pas de bourrée,* etc. 3. A dance by one or more persons; for example, *pas seul* (solo dance), *pas de deux* (dance for two), etc. 4. A group dance; for example, *pas de paysannes* (peasants' dance).

PAS COURU (pah koo-RIU). Literally, running step. 1. A compound *allegro* step, which resembles *pas de bourrée* and is performed very quickly. From the fifth position, step to the second position *demi-pointe* with the front foot, close the other behind in the fifth position on the *demi-pointes;* step to the second position with the front foot, finishing in a *demi-plié* in the second position, with the weight equalized over both feet. This is performed in one musical beat. The step may be finished by an *échappé* into the fifth position or with an *entrechat trois derrière. Pas couru* may be taken *en avant* and *en arrière* as well as *de côté;* in the last case, the feet will open to the fourth position instead of the second position. 2. A running step used to gain momentum for a big leap such as a *grand jeté.*

PAS D'ACTION (pah dahk-SYOn). Literally, dance of action, or action dance. A dance for one or more dancers that conveys a story or expresses an emotion, or in some instances reproduces the movements associated with a particular occupation.

PAS DE BASQUE (pah dih BAHSK). Literally, step of Basque, or Basque step. A basic step of Basque folk dancing that has been adapted to ballet use and is one of the most frequently used steps in the classical repertoire. The *pas de basque* is found in some form in the national, or folk, dances of almost every country. Basically it is a step consisting of three movements: a step to the side; a transference of weight made by crossing the second foot over in front; and another transference of weight to the back foot. In ballet, *pas de basque* takes a number of forms.

Pas de basque en tournant (pah dih bahsk ah*n* toor-NAH*n*). Literally, Basque step turning. A compound step consisting of a *pas de basque sauté en avant,* turning a half turn *en dedans,* and a *pas de basque sauté en arrière,* with a half turn *en dehors* (one complete turn for the whole step).

Pas de basque en tournant, grand (grah*n* pah dih bahsk ah*n* toor-NAH*n*). Literally, large Basque step turning. From the fifth position *demi-plié,* extend the front leg forward to 90°, execute a *demi-grand rond de jambe en dehors,* spring upward, and alight *fondu* on the working foot; execute a *demi-grand rond de jambe en dedans;* turn quickly *en dedans* on the balls of both feet; finish *fondu* in the fifth position.

Pas de basque glissé en avant (pah dih bahsk glee-say ah*n*-nah-VAH*n*). Literally, Basque step gliding forward. From the fifth position *demi-plié,* extend the front foot *pointe tendue devant,* immediately executing a *demi-rond de jambe à terre en dehors;* transfer the weight of the body to the working foot in *demi-plié,* extending the other foot *pointe tendue à la seconde;* slide the pointing foot through the first position *demi-plié* forward to the fourth position *croisé,* remaining in the *demi-plié;* straighten both knees, extending the back foot *pointe tendue croisé derrière;* close to the fifth position *demi-plié.* To perform the *pas de basque glissé en arrière,* reverse all the movements.

Pas de basque, grand (grah*n* pah dih BAHSK). Literally, large Basque step. From the fifth position *demi-plié,* extend the front foot forward at 90°, execute a *demi-grand rond de jambe en dehors,* spring upward, alight *fondu* on the work-

76

ing foot and at the same time execute a *demi-grand rond de jambe en dedans* with the free leg; step forward on the *demi-pointe* of the working foot, and close to the fifth position *demi-plié.*

Pas de basque sauté en avant (pah dih bahsk soh-tay ahn-nah-VAHN). Literally, Basque step jumping. From the fifth position *demi-plié,* extend the front foot forward slightly above the floor and execute a *demi-rond de jambe en dehors, jeté de côté,* and step forward to the *demi-pointe* in the fourth position *croisé, coupé dessous.* To perform the *pas de basque sauté en arrière,* reverse all the movements.

PAS DE BOURRÉE (pah dih boo-RAY). Literally, step of the *bourrée,* or *bourrée* step. The *bourrée* is the native dance of Auvergne, an old province of France. The early ballet masters adapted and refined, for court use, the folk dance movements to provide a basic alphabet of steps. These were later further modified as they were adapted to the classical technique of ballet. The word *bourrée* means "stuffed," and it is possible that the dance derived its name because of its *pas bourrées* or stuffing steps. There are many variations of the *pas de bourrée.*

Pas de bourrée changé (pah dih boo-ray shahn-ZHAY). Literally, *bourrée* step changing. From the fifth position *demi-plié* and raise the back foot *sur le cou-de-pied derrière,* change the weight by stepping onto the *demi-pointe* of the back foot, step with the free foot to the second position on the *demi-pointes,* cross over in front, with the foot which began in the back, sinking in *fondu* and raising the other foot *sur le cou-de-pied derrière.* This step is usually performed in a series, alternating the feet.

Pas de bourrée changé sur les pointes (pah dih boo-ray shahn-zhay siur lay PWANT). Literally, *bourrée* step changing on the toes. From the fifth position *en pointes* or *demi-*

pointes, take a tiny step to the side with the back foot crossing behind, a tiny step to the same side with the front foot, and a tiny step forward with the back foot. This is done very rapidly, remaining on the *pointes* throughout, and alternating sides.

Pas de bourrée couru (pah dih boo-ray koo-RIU). Literally, *bourrée* step running. A series of tiny, very rapid steps performed on the *pointes* or *demi-pointes,* progressing in any given direction; i.e., forward, backward, sideways, obliquely, or in a circle. *Pas de bourrée couru en cinquième* means that the tiny steps are made with the feet maintaining the fifth position on *pointes* or *demi-pointes* throughout the duration of the step. *Pas de bourrée couru en première,* means that the tiny steps are made with the feet together but not turned out, in a position resembling the first position.

Pas de bourrée derrière (pah dih boo-ray dih-ree-AIR). Literally, *bourrée* step in back. This is a *pas de bourrée* performed without a change of feet. From the fifth position *demi-plié* and make a preparatory movement with a *dégagé à la seconde* of the back foot (or the front foot); step across in back of the supporting foot, simultaneously rising to the *demi-pointe* so that the feet are assembled in the fifth position *sur les demi-pointes;* step to the second position *en fondu* with the front foot, simultaneously extending the other foot *pointe tendue à la seconde;* close to the fifth position behind, remaining in the *demi-plié.*

The *pas de bourrée derrière* may also be performed with a step across in back of the supporting foot made on the *demi-pointe,* a step to the second position on the *demi-pointe* with the front foot, and a *coupé dessous* to finish. These are usually performed in a series, advancing or retreating.

Pas de bourrée dessous (pah dih boo-ray dih-soo). Literally, *bourrée* step under. This *pas de bourrée* involves a change of feet. From the fifth position *demi-plié* and make a preparatory movement with a *dégagé à la seconde* of the front foot (or the back foot); step across in back of the supporting foot, simultaneously rising to the *demi-pointe* so that the feet are assembled in the fifth position *sur les demi-pointes;* step to the second position *en fondu* with the front foot, simultaneously extending the other foot *pointe tendue à la seconde;* close to the fifth position in front, remaining in the *demi-plié.*

Pas de bourrée dessus (pah dih boo-ray dih-siu). Literally, *bourrée* step over. This *pas de bourrée* involves a change of feet. From the fifth position *demi-plié* and make a preparatory movement with a *dégagé à la seconde* of the front foot (or the back foot); step across in front of the supporting foot, simultaneously rising to the *demi-pointes* so that the feet are assembled in the fifth position *sur les demi-pointes;* step to the second position *en fondu* with the back foot, the other foot simultaneously *pointe tendue à la seconde;* close to the fifth position in back, remaining in the *demi-plié.*

Pas de bourrée détourné (pah dih boo-ray day-toor-NAY). Literally, *bourrée* step turned aside. See *Pas de bourrée en tournant en dehors.*

Pas de bourrée devant (pah dih boo-ray dih-VAHn). Literally, *bourrée* step in front. This is a *pas de bourrée* performed without a change of feet. From the fifth position *demi-plié* and make a preparatory movement with a *dégagé à la seconde* of the front foot (or the back foot); step across in front of the supporting foot, simultaneously rising to the *demi-pointe* so that the feet are assembled in the fifth position *sur les demi-pointes;* step to the second position *en fondu* with the back foot, simultaneously extending the other foot *pointe tendue à la seconde;* close to the fifth position *demi-plié* in front of the supporting foot.

The *pas de bourrée devant* may also be performed with a step across the supporting foot made on the *demi-pointe,* a step to the second position with the back foot remaining on *demi-pointe,* and a *coupé dessus* to finish. These are usually performed in a series, advancing or retreating.

Pas de bourrée en arrière (pah dih boo-ray ahn-nah-ree-AIR). Literally, *bourrée* step backward. From a position *pointe tendue quatrième devant,* facing either to *effacé* or to *croisé* direction in space, *demi-plié* and rise to the *demi-pointes,* assembling the feet in the fifth position *sur les demi-pointes;* take a small backward step to the fourth position with the back foot, remaining on the *demi-pointes; coupé dessus* with the front foot, finishing in *demi-plié* on the front foot, with the back foot extended *pointe tendue.*

Pas de bourrée en avant (pah dih boo-ray ahn-nah-VAHn). Literally, *bourrée* step forward. From a position *pointe tendue quatrième derrière,* facing either to *effacé* or to *croisé* direction in space, *demi-plié* and rise to the *demi-pointes,* assembling the feet in the fifth position *sur les demi-pointes;* take a small forward step to the fourth position with the front foot, remaining on the *demi-pointes; coupé dessous* with the back foot, finishing in *demi-plié* on the back foot, with the front foot extended *pointe tendue.*

Pas de bourrée en tournant (pah dih boo-ray ahn toor-NAHn). Literally, *bourrée* step turning. This is either a *pas de bourrée dessus* or a *pas de bourrée dessous* performed with a complete turn of the body, either in place or traveling to the side. The *pas de bourrée* may be *fondu* or *piqué* depending on the type of movement desired.

Pas de bourrée en tournant en dedans (pah dih boo-ray ahn toor-nahn ahn dih-DAHn). Literally, *bourrée* step turning inward. This is a *pas de bourrée dessus* performed with a complete turn of the body inward toward the supporting foot. Also called *pas de bourrée dessus en tournant* and *pas de bourrée enveloppé*.

Pas de bourrée en tournant en dehors (pah dih boo-ray ahn toor-nahn ahn dih-OHR). Literally, *bourrée* step turning outward. This is a *pas de bourrée dessous* performed with a complete turn of the body outward toward the foot that initiates the action. Also called *pas de bourrée dessous en tournant* and *pas de bourrée détourné*.

Pas de bourrée fondu (pah dih boo-ray fohn-DIU). Literally, *bourrée* step sinking. A *pas de bourrée* is said to be *fondu* when the second movement (that is, the step to the second position) is made with a *fondu* or sinking action from the *demi-pointe* to the *demi-plié,* remaining in the *demi-plié* for the close in the fifth position.

Pas de bourrée piqué (pah dih boo-ray pee-KAY). Literally, *bourrée* step pricked. A *pas de bourrée* is said to be *piqué* when the feet are sharply picked up with each step. It is performed on the *pointes* or *demi-pointes*.

Pas de bourrée renversé (pah dih boo-ray rahn-vair-SAY). Literally, *bourrée* step turned upside down. A *pas de bourrée en tournant en dehors,* with a back bend and a rotation of the head.

PAS DE CHAT (pah dih SHAH). Literally, step of the cat. A catlike springing step of elevation that may be performed *petit* or *grand.* To perform the *petit pas de chat,* from the fifth position *demi-plié,* raise the back foot *sur le cou-de-pied derrière;* spring lightly upward into the air, raising the other foot to the same height as the first foot; alight *fondu* on the first foot and almost simultaneously close the second foot to the fifth position, remaining in the *demi-*

plié. To perform the *grand pas de chat,* raise the feet *raccourci* and spring higher. *Pas de chat* is also performed with a *dégagé à la seconde* before the *raccourci* movement. Also called *saut de chat.*

Pas de chat jeté (pah dih shah zheh-TAY). Literally, cat step thrown. This is a form of *grand jeté.* A traveling step of high elevation, usually preceded by a preparatory step, such as a *pas couru* or *glissade,* to gain momentum; the back foot is then raised *raccourci* and immediately flung outward; alight on the same foot and pass the other foot forward to the fourth position *croisé en fondu,* weight forward.

Pas de chat russe (pah dih shah ROOSS). Literally, Russian cat step. A name given to a *pas de chat* invented by Michel Fokine for his ballet *Les Sylphides.* From the fifth position *en croisé, demi-plié,* brush the back foot into a half *attitude* position behind the supporting leg, spring lightly into the air, alight *fondu* on the first foot and immediately pass the other foot forward, finishing in the fourth position *croisé en fondu,* arms *à deux bras.*

Pas de chat russe, grand (grah*n* pah dih shah ROOSS). Literally, large Russian cat step. A traveling step of high elevation usually preceded by a preparatory step such as a *pas couru,* a *glissade,* or a *failli.* To gain momentum, the back foot is thrown forward high into the air as for a *grand jeté;* this is followed immediately by a *raccourci* movement. Alight on the same foot and immediately pass the other foot through the first position to the fourth position *croisé en fondu,* with the weight forward and the back knee straight.

PAS DE CHEVAL (pah dih shih-VAHL). Literally, step of the horse: so called because the movement of the foot resembles the movement made by a horse when it paws the ground. From a position *pointe tendue devant* brush the

pointing foot inward toward the supporting knee, *développé devant,* and return to *pointe tendue devant.* The
step is usually performed in a series alternating feet and
lightly springing from foot to foot on the *pointes* or *demi-
pointes.*

PAS DE CISEAUX (pah dih see-ZOH). Literally, scissors step.
See *Ciseaux, pas de.*

PAS DE DEUX (pah dih DUH). A dance for two people.

Pas de deux, grand (grahn pah dih DUH). Literally, grand
dance for two. The name given to the bravura dance performed by the ballerina and her cavalier. In the traditional
romantic (so-called classical) ballets the *grand pas de deux*
is the high point of the ballet. Traditionally, the *grand pas
de deux* consists of five parts: the *entrée,* or entrance; the
adage in which the male *danseur* (cavalier) supports the
danseuse (ballerina) in long sustained poses, multiple
pirouettes, and high lifts; the solo variation for the *danseur;*
the solo variation for the *danseuse;* and the coda, or climax
of the dance, in which both dancers dance together and
take turns at performing individually the most complex
virtuoso steps.

PAS DE POISSON (pah dih pwah-SOHn). Literally, fish step.
See *Temps de poisson.*

PAS DE QUATRE (pah dih KAH-trih). A dance for four
people. The most famous *pas de quatre* in ballet history
took place in London on July 12, 1845, at a command
performance for Queen Victoria. Danced by the four greatest *ballerinas* of the nineteenth century, Marie Taglioni,
Carlotta Grisi, Fanny Cerrito, and Lucille Grahn, this un-
usual event generated excitement that still echoes today
in the world of the ballet.

PAS DE TROIS (pah dih TRWAH). A dance for three people.

PAS DE VALSE (pah dih VAHLS). Waltz step. A step consisting of three movements—glide, step, change—performed to three-quarter time, with a slow turn.

PAS GLISSÉ (pah glee-SAY). Literally, gliding step. Any step that glides on the floor; for example, the *glissade* and *pas de basque glissé*.

PAS MARCHÉ (pah mahr-SHAY). Literally, walking step. 1. Any dignified walking step. 2. A walking step preceded by a *développé devant en fondu*. It may be performed on the whole foot or with *piqué* and *fondu*.

PASSÉ (pah-SAY). Literally, passed. A traditional movement used in passing from one position to another. The point of the working foot passes the supporting knee on its way to its ultimate position. For example, *relevé passé en arrière*.

PASSE-PIED (pahss pee-AY). Literally, foot passing. A kind of small *jeté* alternating the feet, finishing *pointe tendue à terre*. From the fifth position *demi-plié* make a tiny spring upward and simultaneously *développé* the front foot to the fourth position front; alight *fondu* with the toes pointed on the floor. With a little spring change feet. Continue the springing change of feet as many times as desired. *Passe-pied* may be performed *devant, derrière,* and *de côté*.

PAS SEUL (pah SUHL). A dance for one, or solo dance.

PAS TOMBÉ (pah tohn-BAY). Literally, falling step. A movement in which the dancer allows the weight to fall on one foot, forward, backward, or sideways. It may be a preparatory movement used to transfer the weight before a *développé* or *sauté*, or a part of a compound step such as *sissonne tombée*.

PENCHÉ (pahn-SHAY), **PENCHÉE** (pahn-SHAY). Literally, leaning. A term used to indicate that the body leans for-

84

ward or backward and the working foot is raised high so that the toe of the foot is the highest point; for example, *arabesque penchée.*

PETIT (p'tee), **PETITE** (p'teet). Small; little; short.

PETITS TOURS (p'tee TOOR). Small turns. See *Tours,* *chaînés,* and *Déboulés.*

PIED À DEMI (pee-ay ah d'MEE). Literally, foot on the half. A position of the foot at half the distance between the whole foot resting on the floor and the point position, with the weight of the body resting on the ball of one foot, the heel lifted off the floor.

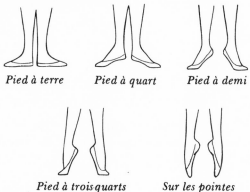

Pied à terre   *Pied à quart*   *Pied à demi*

Pied à trois quarts   *Sur les pointes*

PIED À QUART (pee-ay ah KAHR). Literally, foot on the quarter. A position of the foot at a quarter of the distance between the whole foot resting on the floor and the point position, with the weight of the body resting on the ball of one foot, the heel lifted off the floor.

PIED À TERRE (pee-ay ah TAIR). Literally, foot on the ground. A position of the foot in which the entire sole of the foot rests on the floor.

PIED À TROIS QUARTS (pee-ay ah trwah KAHR). Literally, foot on the three quarters. A position of the foot at three quarters of the distance between the whole foot resting on the floor and the point position, with the weight of the body resting high on the ball of one foot, the heel lifted off the floor.

PIED, ÊTRE DE (eh-trih dih pee-AY). Literally, to be of foot. A term used to signify that at the end of an *enchaînement* the dancer is correctly placed in order to begin the next movement.

PIEDS, CINQ POSITIONS DES (sank poh-zee-syon day pee-AY). The five positions of the feet. These positions have remained the fundamental basis for all movements of the feet since the basic rules for ballet technique were laid down by Pierre Beauchamp toward the end of the seventeenth century (see also *Beauchamp, Pierre*).

Première position (first position): the legs are turned outward at the thighs so that the feet are turned outward at an angle of 180°, with the heels touching each other.

Seconde position (second position): the legs and feet are turned outward, as for the first position, but the heels are about one foot apart.

Troisième position (third position): the legs and feet are turned outward as for the first position, the feet are close together and crossed over so that the front foot forms a right angle to the instep of the supporting foot.

Quatrième position (fourth position): there are two variations of the fourth position, *ouverte* and *croisée*. *Quatrième position ouverte* (open fourth position): in this position the feet do not cross over each other. The open fourth is taken from the first position, with the legs and feet turned outward at 180°, one foot forward at a distance of about a foot from the other. *Quatrième position croisée* (crossed fourth position): today the crossed fourth position

Première position	Seconde position	Troisième position	Quatrième position ouverte	Quatrième position croisée	Cinquième position

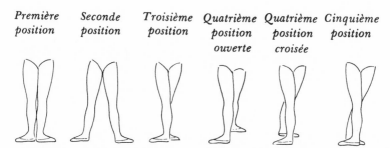

is taken from the fifth position, although formerly it was taken from the third position. The legs and feet are turned outward at 180°, one foot in front of the other and parallel at a distance of about a foot.

Cinquième position (fifth position): the legs and feet are turned out at 180°, the feet parallel and close together, one foot crossed over the other, with the heel of the front foot at the joint of the big toe of the back foot.

The positions of the feet may also be performed *sur les demi-pointes* and *sur les pointes*. The open positions (second and fourth) may also be performed *en l'air* (at 90°) or *à la demi-hauteur* (at 45°).

PIÉTINER (pee-ay-tih-NAY). Literally, to stamp the feet. A term applied to accented movements *sur les pointes*.

PIQUÉ (pee-KAY). Literally, pricked or pricking. 1. A step in which the body shoots sharply in any given direction (*devant, derrière,* or *de côté*) and the step is made directly to the *pointe* or *demi-pointe* of the supporting foot, with the other foot being raised in any desired position. Also called *posé*. 2. A sharp, picked-up action of the feet, in which the performer steps on *pointes* or *demi-pointes;* for example, *pas de bourrée piqué*. 3. A movement finished *pointe tendue;* for example, *battements piqués*.

PIQUÉ À TERRE (pee-kay ah TAIR). Literally, pricking the ground. See *Pointe tendue à terre*.

PIQUÉ DÉTOURNÉ (pee-kay day-toor-NAY). Literally, pricking turn aside. From the fifth position *demi-plié*, *dégagé* the back foot *à la seconde,* and step to the *pointe* or *demi-pointe;* immediately cross the other foot behind in the fifth position *sur les pointes* or *demi-pointes* and turn outward.

PIQUÉ ENVELOPPÉ (pee-kay ahn-vloh-PAY). Literally, pricking enveloping. See *Tour de basque.*

PIQUER LA POINTE (pee-kay lah PWAHnT). Literally, to prod the toe. A term used to indicate that the working foot is stretched *pointe tendue* in any given direction and that the toe strikes the floor lightly.

PIQUÉ TOUR (pee-kay TOOR). Literally, pricking turn. A *pirouette* performed either *en dehors* or *en dedans,* in any given position, made by stepping directly to the *pointe* or *demi-pointe* of the working foot. Also called *posé tour* and *piqué tourné.*

Piqué tour en dedans (pee-kay toor ahn dih-DAHn). Literally, pricking turn inward. From the fifth position *demi-plié, dégagé* the front foot *devant,* and immediately execute a *demi-rond de jambe en dehors;* step on the *pointe* or *demi-pointe* to the second position, raising the other foot to the *cou-de-pied derrière* (or *devant*); execute one or more turns in the same line of direction; finish with a *coupé dessous.* It may also be performed with the raised leg in the *arabesque* or *attitude* position and may finish with a *fondu* of the supporting foot.

Piqué tour en dehors (pee-kay toor ahn dih-OHR). Literally, pricking turn outward. From the fourth position *pointe tendue devant, à terre, demi-plié* and immediately execute a *demi-rond de jambe en dehors;* step *fondu* to the second

88

position; cross the other foot over in front, stepping on the *pointe* or *demi-pointe,* raising the free foot *sur le cou-de-pied devant;* execute one or more turns in the same line of direction; finish with a *tombé à la seconde.* It may also be performed with the raised leg in the *arabesque* or *attitude* position and may finish with a *fondu* of the supporting foot.

PIROUETTE (peer-oo-WET). Literally, whirl. A complete turn of the body on one foot, usually on the *demi-pointe* or *pointe.* A proficient technician makes multiple turns, some dancers having achieved as many as fifteen or sixteen revolutions from one preparation. *Pirouettes* may be performed in any given position, that is, *sur le cou-de-pied, en arabesque, en attitude, à la seconde,* etc. *Pirouettes* are performed *en dehors,* turning outward in the direction of the raised leg, or *en dedans,* turning inward in the direction of the supporting leg.

Pirouette, grande (grahnd peer-oo-WET). Literally, great whirl. Any series of bravura turns on one foot, such as a series of turns with the free leg held *à la seconde position en l'air,* or *en attitude,* or in combined positions. The *grande pirouette* may include hopping turns as well as *relevé* turns and is usually performed to sixteen or thirty-two measures of galop (two-quarter) music, ending with multiple turns *sur le cou-de-pied.*

Pirouette renversée (peer-oo-wet rahn-vair-SAY). Literally, whirl upset. A *pirouette* performed *en dedans,* with the raised leg *raccourci.* Make two complete turns of the body. At the beginning of the second turn, bend the body to the side of the raised leg; at the end of the turn, bend the body forcefully to the side of the supporting leg, while throwing open the raised leg with a *développé à la seconde.*

PISTOLET (pees-toh-LAY). Literally, pistol. See *Ailes de pigeons.*

PLACÉ (plah-SAY). Literally, placed; placement. A term used to indicate that the dancer's aplomb is correct; that is, the body is centered with the head, shoulders, hips, and limbs correctly aligned to one another. A dancer is said to be *bien placé* (well placed) when able to maintain perfect aplomb and correct alignment while moving.

PLACEMENT, BODY. See *Placé.*

PLACE, SUR (siur PLAHS). Literally, on place. A term used to indicate that in executing a certain step the dancer remains in the same place without traveling in any direction.

Bien placé

PLANÉ (plah-NAY). Literally, soared; hovered. A term used to describe any elevation movement or step in which the dancer tries to remain in the air as long as possible.

PLIÉ (plee-AY). Literally, bent; bending. A bending movement of the knees. The *plié* underlies all steps and movements of ballet and lends lightness and softness to all movements and jumps. A good *plié* has an elastic quality.

Plié, grand (grahn plee-AY). A complete bending of the knees until the thighs are in a horizontal position, the body remaining upright. The heels are raised in the first, third, fourth, and fifth positions; the heels remain securely on the floor in the second position.

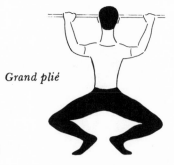

Grand plié

POINTES, SUR LES (siur lay PWAHnt). On the points, or tips of the toes. This is the full point position.

90

Première
position

Seconde
position

Quatrième
position

Cinquième
position

SUR LES POINTES

POINTES, TEMPS DE (tah*n* dih PWAH*n*T). Movements on the points. The generic term for all steps executed on the toes, or full point position.

POINTE TENDUE (pwah*n*t tah*n*-DIU). Literally, point stretched. A term used to indicate that the foot is pointed; that is, the instep is stretched and the toes are pressed downward, the weight of the body being supported by the other foot.

Pointe tendue à terre (pwah*n*t tah*n*-diu ah TAIR). Literally, foot pointed on the ground. The tips of the toes of the pointed foot rest lightly on the floor. Also called *piqué à terre* (French school) and *dégagé*.

POINT WORK. Dancing on the tips of the toes. See *Pointes, sur les.*

PORT DE BRAS (por dih BRAH). Literally, carriage of the arms. 1. The generic term for any movement of the arms in ballet. 2. The generic term for the exercises of the arms designed to make them move gracefully and harmoniously while maintaining the prescribed form of ballet. It is interesting to note that originally the term was *corps et bras* and that through usage the term has been corrupted to *port de bras.*

PORTÉ (por-TAY). Literally, carried. 1. A term used to indicate that a step travels from one place to another, for example, *assemblé porté*. 2. The lifting and carrying of the *ballerina* by her partner.

POSE (pohz). A fixed position; arrangement of posture.

POSÉ (poh-ZAY). Literally, poised. See *Piqué*.

POSER (poh-ZAY). Literally, to place. To place the foot on the floor.

POSITION FERMÉE (poh-zee-syon fair-MAY). Literally, closed position. A position in which the feet touch each other. The first, third, and fifth positions of the feet are *positions fermées*.

POSITION OUVERTE (poh-zee-syon oo-VAIRT). Literally, open position. A position in which the feet are held apart. The second and the fourth positions of the feet are *positions ouvertes*.

POSITIONS OF THE ARMS. See *Bras, positions de*.

POSITIONS OF THE BODY. There are eleven basic positions of the body as it turns to various directions in space. These are *croisé devant* and *croisé derrière, à la quatrième devant* and *à la quatrième derrière, écarté devant* and *écarté derrière, effacé devant* and *effacé derrière, à la seconde, épaulé devant* and *derrière*. See illustrations under each entry and frontispiece diagram.

POSITIONS OF THE FEET. See *Pieds, cinq positions des*.

POSITIONS OF THE HEAD. The head assumes five different positions in ballet—erect, inclined, turned, lowered, and raised.

POSITIONS SOULEVÉES (poh-zee-syon soo-leh-VAY). Literally, raised positions. A term used to refer to the open positions (*positions ouvertes*) of the feet, *pointe tendue* and *en l'air* (French school).

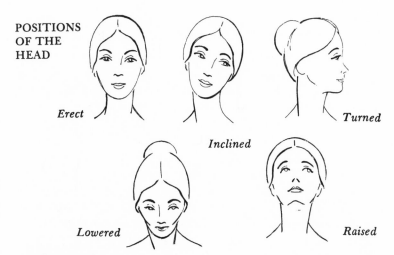

POSITIONS OF THE HEAD

Erect

Turned

Inclined

Lowered

Raised

PRÉCIPITÉ (pray-see-pee-TAY). Literally, hurling; hurrying; accelerating. A form of the step *glissade*. See *Glissade précipité*.

PREMIER (prehm-YAY), **PREMIÈRE** (prehm-YAIR). First.

PREMIÈRE, EN (ahn prehm-YAIR). In the first; that is, in the first position.

PREOBRAJENSKAYA, OLGA (OHL-gah pray-oh-brah-JEHN-skah-yah), 1871–1964. She was born in St. Petersburg, Russia, and became *prima ballerina* of the Imperial Ballet, one of the brightest stars of the Russian stage during the latter part of the nineteenth century and early twentieth. She was the recipient of two gold medals from the Ministry of the Court. From 1917 to 1921 she taught at the State School of Ballet, Petrograd (formerly the Imperial school in St. Petersburg). In 1921 she left Russia to make her home in Paris where she taught privately until she died, becoming one of the world's most renowned teachers of ballet. See *Brisé télémaque*.

PRÉPARATION (pray-pah-rah-syon). Preparation. The preparatory movement for a step or turn.

93

PROMENADE, EN (ah*n* prohm-NAHD). Literally, in a walk. A term used to indicate that the dancer revolves slowly in place while maintaining a definite pose. It may be performed by the dancer, male or female, alone, without assistance, by slight movements of the heel. In a *pas de deux* the *ballerina* is turned by her partner, who circles around her, holding one (or both) of her hands.

𝒬

QUADRILLE (kah-DREEL). 1. A French dance of the early nineteenth century, performed by two or four couples moving in a square. 2. Derived from the Italian *quadrighia,* a little troop. A term used of a group of dancers; for example, *première quadrille, seconde quadrille.*

QUARRÉ, EN (ah*n* kah-RAY). See *En carré.*

QUART (kahr). A quarter; for example, *un quart de tour.*

QUATRE (KAH-trih). Four.

QUATRIÈME (kah-tree-EHM). Fourth.

QUATRIÈME DERRIÈRE, À LA (ah lah kah-tree-ehm dih-ree-AIR). To the fourth position back; for example, *battement tendu à la quatrième derrière,* and *développé à la quatrième derrière.*

QUATRIÈME DERRIÈRE, GRANDE (grahnd kah-tree-ehm dih-ree-AIR). Large fourth position back. A term used to indicate that the back leg is raised.

QUATRIÈME DEVANT, À LA (ah lah kah-tree-ehm dih-VAHn). To the fourth position front; for example, *battement tendu à la quatrième devant,* and *développé à la quatrième devant.*

QUATRIÈME DEVANT, GRANDE (grahnd kah-tree-ehm dih-VAHn). Large fourth position front. A term used to indicate that the front leg is raised.

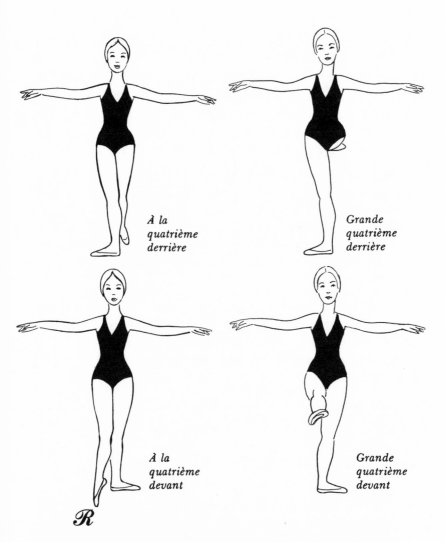

*À la
quatrième
derrière*

*Grande
quatrième
derrière*

*À la
quatrième
devant*

*Grande
quatrième
devant*

$\mathscr{R}$

RACCOURCI (rah-koor-SEE). Literally, shortened. Short and sharp. 1. A position of the working leg in which the thigh is raised parallel to the floor (*à la seconde position*), with the knee sharply bent and the pointed toes resting at the knee of the supporting leg. Also called *retiré*. 2. A short, sharp bending movement of the knee, for example, *fouetté raccourci*.

RAMASSÉ (rah-mah-SAY). Picked up; picking up.

RECULANT, EN (ahn rih-kiu-LAHn). Literally, drawing back. A term used to indicate that the working leg passes from front to back, causing the dancer to move from the front of the stage (downstage) to the back of the stage (upstage). For example, *emboîté en reculant* (French school).

RELEVÉ (rih-leh-VAY). Literally, relifted. A term used to indicate that the body is raised to the full point or half point during the execution of a step or movement. It also may refer to the lowering of the heel of the working foot from a *pointe tendue* position to the floor and reraising it to the *pointe tendue* position. For example, *battement relevé*.

Relevé derrière (rih-leh-vay dih-ree-AIR). From the fifth position, a rising or springing to the half point, or full point, of the front foot as the back foot is simultaneously raised behind the ankle, or knee, of the supporting leg. See *Retiré, temps*.

Relevé devant (rih-leh-vay dih-VAHn). From the fifth position, a rising or springing to the half point, or full point, of the back foot as the front foot is simultaneously raised in front of the ankle, or knee, of the supporting leg. See *Retiré, temps*.

Relevé passé (rih-leh-vay pah-SAY). A step similar to the *relevé devant* and *relevé derrière* except that the working foot passes from front to back, when the movement is known as *relevé passé en arrière*, or from back to front, when it is called *relevé passé en avant*. See *Retiré, temps*.

RELEVÉ, TEMPS (tahn rih-leh-VAY). Literally, time relifted or raising movement. A raising of the body to the half-point or full-point position on one or both feet. *Temps re-*

96

levé may be performed in any given pose; that is, *relevé en arabesque, relevé en attitude.* Through usage the term *temps relevé* has been shortened to *relevé.*

REMONTANT, EN (ah*n* rih-mohn-TAH*n*). Literally, going up. A term used to indicate that the working leg moves from front to back, causing the dancer to move from the front of the stage (downstage) to the back of the stage (upstage). For example, *assemblé en remontant.*

RENVERSÉ (rahn-vair-SAY), **RENVERSÉE** (rahn-vair-SAY). Literally, upset; reversed. A movement of the body during a turn in which the normal balance is upset by bending sideways and back without disturbing the equilibrium. *Renversé* may be performed *en dehors* and *en dedans, relevé* or *sauté.* The step *renversé* takes several different forms when performed *en dehors.* It may be executed with a turn on one foot in an *attitude* position or a turn on both feet. Some *renversés* finish with a *pas de bourrée.*

En dehors: 1. After a preparatory *failli* or *coupé dessus; coupé dessous* throwing the free leg up to *croisé devant en l'air,* immediately execute a *grand rond de jambe en dehors* simultaneously executing a *relevé* with the supporting foot. The *rond de jambe* terminates in *attitude fondue* and the step is finished with a *pas de bourrée en tournant en dehors.* The arms execute a *port de bras* through the fifth position front to the third position high (the high arm corresponds to the working leg), culminating with a downward circular movement of the high arm to finish in the fifth position low. 2. After a preparatory *failli* or *coupé dessus; coupé dessous* carrying the arms to the fifth position front, spring lightly to the *demi-pointe* executing a *grand rond de jambe* with the free leg as the corresponding arm is lifted to the third position high, immediately place the working foot behind the supporting foot in the fifth position *sur les demi-pointes, détourné,* and finish with *coupé dessous* as the arm circles downward in front of the face. 3. After a preparatory *failli* or *coupé dessus; coupé dessous* and execute a *grand rond de jambe en dehors* and at the same time *relevé* on the supporting foot, turning the body *en dehors* and raising the arm (which corresponds to the supporting leg) to the third position high. As the body faces the back of the stage the working leg is forcibly bent to *attitude* and the upper body is thrown back into a deep bend. The movement culminates by completing the turn (one complete turn) and executing a *fondu* with the supporting leg.

En dedans: From *arabesque ouverte croisée; demi-plié* and draw the working leg sharply *raccourci,* simultaneously bend the body forcibly from the waist toward the working knee, *relevé* on the supporting foot, turning one turn *en dedans,* and finish the turn with a throwing movement of the working foot to the second position *en l'air.* As the foot extends to the open position, the body is forcibly bent to the opposite side while remaining on the *pointe* or *demi-pointe* of the supporting foot.

RÉPÉTER (ray-pay-TAY). Literally, to repeat. To practice or rehearse.

RÉPÉTITION (ray-pay-tee-SYO*n*). Rehearsal.

RETIRÉ, TEMPS (tah*n* rih-tih-RAY). Literally, time withdrawn, or withdrawing movement. A movement in which the knee of the working leg is drawn up so that the thigh is opened outward to the second position in the air, parallel to the floor, with the toes of the working foot pointing at the supporting knee. Through usage the term has been shortened to *retiré.* Also called *raccourci.*

Retiré, battement (baht-mah*n* rih-tih-RAY). See *Battement retiré.*

98

Retiré sauté (rih-tih-ray soh-TAY). Literally, withdrawing movement jumped. A step of high elevation in which the *retiré* movement is performed while the dancer springs high into the air. It may be performed *en arrière* (front foot raised up to the knee and closed behind in the fifth position on alighting), or *en avant* (back foot raised up to the knee and closed in front in the fifth position on alighting).

RÉVÉRENCE (ray-vay-RAHns). Literally, reverence. Curtsey; bow.

ROND (rohn). Round; circular; circle.

ROND, EN (ahn ROHn). In a circle; for example, *battement en rond.* See *Battement arrondi.*

ROND DE JAMBE (rohn dih ZHAHnb). Literally, circle of the leg.

Rond de jambe à terre (rohn dih zhahnb ah TAIR). Literally, circle of the leg on the ground. It may be performed *en dehors* or *en dedans.* For *en dehors:* the working foot extends, *pointe tendue,* to the fourth position front, describes an arc or semicircle passing through the second position (*pointe tendue*), finishing *pointe tendue* in the fourth position back. The toes glide on the floor. The working foot may then be closed to the fifth position behind (*rond de jambe à terre fermé*), or it may pass through the first position to repeat the circle any desired number of times. Both knees remain tightly pulled up throughout the movements. To perform the *rond de jambe à terre en dedans,* reverse the movements.

Rond de jambe à terre, demi-grand (d'mee grahn rohn dih zhahnb ah TAIR). The same as *demi-rond de jambe à terre,* except that it is performed with the supporting knee bent in *demi-plié.* See *Demi-rond de jambe à terre.*

Rond de jambe à terre, grand (grahn rohn dih zhahnb ah TAIR). Literally, large circle of the leg on the ground. The supporting knee is bent in *demi-plié* while the working foot executes a semicircle on the floor, either *en dehors* or *en dedans*. Because the supporting knee is bent, the arc described by the working foot will be larger and extended farther out from the body.

Rond de jambe en l'air (rohn dih zhahnb ahn LAIR). Literally, circle of the leg in the air. A circular (elliptical) movement of the foot performed with the thigh of the working leg held in the second position in the air, either at 90° or 45°. *Ronds de jambe en l'air* may be performed *en dehors* (the foot circles outward toward the back) or *en dedans* (the foot circles inward toward the front). With each circle the movement ends with the leg extended in the second position in the air. It may be performed slowly or rapidly, with one circle for each musical beat or two or more circles for each beat. It may be performed on the whole supporting foot or the *demi-pointe, piqué, relevé,* or *sauté.*

Rond de jambe en l'air, demi-grand (d'mee grahn rohn dih zhahnb ahn LAIR). The toes of the working foot describe an arc from the fourth position, front, in the air to the second position in the air (*en dehors*), or from the fourth position, back, in the air to the second position in the air (*en dedans*). It may be performed at 90° or *à la demi-hauteur.*

Rond de jambe en l'air, grand (grahn rohn dih zhahnb ahn LAIR). Literally, large circle of the leg in the air. The toes of the working foot describe an arc, or semicircle, in the air, in the same manner as they describe the semicircle on the floor in the *rond de jambe à terre*. It may be performed *en dehors* or *en dedans,* at 90° or *à la demi-hauteur.*

100

Rond de jambe en l'air sauté (rohn dih zhahnb ahn lair soh-TAY). Literally, circle of the leg in the air jumping. The *rond de jambe en l'air* is executed while the supporting foot makes a *temps levé* or spring into the air. It may be performed *en dehors* or *en dedans* in a single or double *rond de jambe.*

Rond de jambe fermé (rohn dih zhahnb fair-MAY). Literally, circle of the leg closed. A *rond de jambe* is said to be *fermé,* or closed, when the working foot finishes the circle by closing to the fifth position.

Rond de jambe jeté en l'air (rohn dih zhahnb zheh-tay ahn LAIR). Literally, circle of the leg thrown in the air. A form of *grand rond de jambe en l'air* in which the working knee is raised in a half-bent position forward (or backward) and thrown open to the second position before being carried back (or front) to the fourth position. It may be performed *en dehors* or *en dedans.*

Rond de jambe ouvert (rohn dih zhahnb oo-VAIR). Literally, circle of the leg open. A *rond de jambe* is said to be *ouvert,* or open, when the working foot finishes the circle open in the second position.

Rond de jambe piqué (rohn dih zhahnb pee-KAY). Literally, circle of the leg pricked. The *rond de jambe* is said to be *piqué* when the toes are lifted in the air, striking the floor lightly at each point of the semicircle, fourth front, second, fourth back, or vice versa.

Ronds de jambe balancé (rohn dih zhahnb bah-lahn-SAY). Literally, circles of the leg balanced. A series of *grands ronds de jambe* performed rapidly, alternately *en dehors* and *en dedans.* The working leg swings backward and forward, the toes describing arcs in the air.

Ronds de jambe en l'air entournant (roh*n* dih zhah*n*b ah*n* lair ah*n* toor-NAH*n*). Literally, circles of the leg in the air turning. A series of *ronds de jambe en l'air* (either *en dehors* or *en dedans*) performed while the supporting foot slowly turns (*promenade*), causing the dancer to revolve in place.

RONDS DE BRAS (roh*n* dih BRAH). Literally, circles of the arms.

ROTATION (roh-tah-SYO*n*). The rotating of the leg in the hip socket in movements where the body turns with a pivot on the supporting foot while the working foot remains in its former position.

ROYALE (rwah-YAL). Literally, royal. A special term for the *changement battu* or beaten *changement*. The dancer strikes the calves of the legs together before making the change of feet in the air.

ROYALE DOUBLE (rwah-yal DOO-blih). Literally, double royal. The calves of the legs are struck together twice. From the fifth position *demi-plié,* spring into the air, strike the legs against each other, keeping the same foot in front, strike the legs together again as in *entrechat quatre,* and finish with the same foot in front.

Royale double fermé (rwah-yal doo-blih fair-MAY). From *demi-plié* in the second position spring into the air, cross the feet in the fifth position, open to small second, cross the feet again in the fifth position with a change of feet, open to a small second and finish in the fifth position *fondu.* Also called *entrechat cinq fermé.*

Royale double ouvert (rwah-yal doo-blih oo-VAIR). This is performed with the same beat as in *royale double* but finish in the second position *fondu.* Also called *entrechat cinq ouvert.*

102

RUSSIAN SCHOOL. Historically the ballet academy of Russia dates from 1738. Credit for the artistic development and growth of the school begins with the Frenchman, Charles LePicq, who first came to Russia in 1786 as *premier danseur*. Later as chief ballet master and choreographer, this pupil of Noverre, following the precepts of his master, did much to develop the native talent. In 1801 Charles Didelot began a long tenure as choreographer for the Imperial Ballet. He is credited as being the father of the present Russian school, setting up the system of teaching which still underlies Russian training. In 1860 Christian Johannsen began a reign as chief teacher of the Imperial school which lasted for nearly half a century.

LePicq had been a pupil of Noverre; Didelot a pupil of Dauberval (himself a pupil of Noverre), Auguste Vestris, and Noverre; Johannsen carried on the same tradition, being a pupil of August Bournonville who had been a pupil of Vestris and other famous French teachers, including his own father who had been a pupil of Noverre.

The Russian school was founded on the French which stressed grace, charm, and elegance. However, in 1885 the guest appearance in Russia of Virginia Zucchi, a pupil of Carlo Blasis in Italy, created such a stir because of the technical virtuosity displayed by the dancer that the Russian dancers hastened to emulate her training. The subsequent appearance in 1887 of other brilliant Italian dancers such as Enrico Cecchetti (a pupil of Lepri who had been a pupil of Blasis) intensified the drive for more strength, vigor, and brilliance of technique. Nicolas Legat in his book *The Story of the Russian School* says of the training and style which we have come to know as "the Russian School": "The secret of the development of Russian dancing lay in the fact that we learnt from everybody and adapted what we learnt to ourselves. We copied, borrowed from, and emulated every source that gave us inspiration, and then,

103

working from our acquired knowledge and lending it the stamp of the Russian national genius, we molded it into the eclectic art of the Russian ballet . . . it was our refusal to sacrifice aesthetics to effect, combined with our success in adopting and adapting Italian technique that enabled us in the generation that followed the arrival of the Italians in Russia to produce the greatest dancers of the past four decades."

The method of training today in Soviet Russia remains based on these eternally true principles revitalized by Agrippina Vaganova.

$\mathscr{S}$

SALLE, AU TOUR DE LA (oh toor dih lah SAHL). Around the room.

SAUT DE BASQUE (soh dih BAHSK). Literally, jump of Basque, or Basque jump. A traveling turning step, usually of high elevation, although it may also be performed low to the floor. *Demi-plié* and step out to the second position with the right foot; spring into the air, simultaneously turning a half turn *en dedans* and throwing both legs to the second position; finish by completing the turn to face front, alighting on the left foot, *fondu*, with the right leg bent in *raccourci devant*. *Saut de basque* is also performed with a double turn in the air, or *battu* (with beats), by beating the legs together the number of times desired— once, twice, or three times—as the turn is being made.

SAUT DE CHAT (soh dih SHAH). See *Pas de chat.*

SAUT DE FLÈCHE (soh dih FLESH). See *Temps de flèche.*

SAUTÉ (soh-TAY). Jumped or jumping; for example, *échappé sauté.*

SCÈNE (sehn). Stage.

SCÈNE D'ACTION (sehn dahk-SYOn). Literally, scene of action. A mimed scene or episode in a *ballet d'action*, or story ballet. The *scène d'action* was an important part of the romantic ballets of the nineteenth century.

SECOND (seh-GOHn), **SECONDE** (seh-GOHnD). Second.

SECONDE, À LA (ah lah seh-GOHnD). Literally, to the second. To the second position; for example, *développé à la seconde* and *pointe tendue à la seconde*.

SECONDE, EN (ahn seh-GOHnD). Literally, in the second. In the second position; for example, *plié en seconde*.

SECONDE, GRANDE (grahnd seh-GOHnD). Literally, large second. A term used to indicate that the leg is in second position in the air.

Grande seconde

SEPT (set). Seven.

SERRÉ (seh-RAY). Close; compact; tight; concise. For example, *petits battements serrés*.

SERRER LES REINS (seh-ray lay RIHn). Literally, to tighten the loins. A term used in teaching ballet to indicate that the buttocks muscles should be tightened and the torso well lifted out of the hips with the abdominal muscles tightening toward the spine.

SIDE PRACTICE. A term for exercises at the *barre*. See *Exercices à la barre*.

SIMPLE (SAn-plih). Literally, simple or ordinary, as in *sissonne simple*.

105

SISOL (see-SOHL). A corruption of the term *sissonne*. Although occasionally used by some teachers, this is an incorrect term.

SISSONNE, PAS (pah see-SOHn). Derived from the name of its inventor, the Comte de Sissonne. There are a number of variations of the basic step, which is a jump from two feet onto one foot.

Sissonne battue (see-sohn bah-TIU). Beaten *sissonne*. *Sissonne simple, sissonne fermée,* and *sissonne ouverte* may all be performed with beats. *Sissonne simple battue* is also called *entrechat trois* or *entrechat cinq,* depending on the number of beats performed. *Sissonne fermée battue* is performed with an *entrechat quatre* beat and is also called *entrechat cinq ramassé.* It may be made *en avant* or *en arrière.* When made *de côté* it is performed with a *royale* or a *royale double* beat. *Sissonne ouverte battue* may be performed with an *entrechat trois, cinq,* or *sept* beat.

Sissonne changée (see-sohn shahn-ZHAY). *Sissonne* changing (feet). The *sissonne changée* may be *fermée* or *fondue.* The term is applied to a *sissonne en avant* or *en arrière* with a change of feet. For *sissonne changée en avant,* from the fifth position *demi-plié,* spring into the air, traveling forward and throwing the feet apart to the fourth position, passing the back foot forward; alight on the foot that came forward and close the other foot behind in the fifth position. For *sissonne changée en arrière,* from the fifth position *demi-plié,* spring in the air traveling backward and throwing the feet apart to the fourth position passing the front foot back; alight on the foot that passed back and close the other foot front in the fifth position.

Sissonne doublée (see-sohn doo-BLAY). *Sissonne* doubled. A compound step consisting of a *sissonne ouverte de côté,* a *coupé,* and an *assemblé.* It may be performed *dessous* or *dessus.* For *dessous,* from the fifth position *demi-plié, sissonne ouverte de côté* direction of front foot, *coupé dessous, assemblé dessous.* For *dessus,* from the fifth position *demi-plié, sissonne ouverte de côté* direction of back foot, *coupé dessus; assemblé dessus.* Also called *sissonne retombée* (Cecchetti method).

Sissonne fermée (see-sohn fair-MAY). Closed *sissonne.* A traveling step performed to a quick tempo with small elevation. It may be performed *en avant, en arrière,* and *de côté,* in any given direction in space, that is, *croisé, effacé, écarté,* and so on. For *sissonne fermée en avant,* from the fifth position *demi-plié,* spring into the air traveling forward and throwing the feet apart to the fourth position; alight on the front foot, *fondu,* and almost simultaneously close the back foot into the fifth position, remaining in the *demi-plié* and gliding the foot on the floor. For *sissonne fermée en arrière,* from the fifth position *demi-plié,* spring into the air, traveling backward and throwing the feet apart to the fourth position; alight on the back foot, *fondu,* and almost simultaneously close the front foot into the fifth position, remaining in the *demi-plié* and gliding the foot on the floor.

The *sissonne fermée de côté* may be performed *dessus, dessous,* or without a change of feet. For *dessus,* from the fifth position *demi-plié,* spring into the air, traveling to the side in the direction of the front foot and throwing the feet apart to the second position; alight on the front foot, *fondu,* and almost simultaneously close the other foot front in the fifth position, remaining in the *demi-plié* and gliding it on the floor. For *dessous,* from the fifth position *demi-plié,* spring into the air, traveling to the side in the direction of the back foot, and throwing the feet apart to the second position; alight on the back foot, *fondu,* and almost simultaneously close the other foot behind in the fifth position, remaining in the *demi-plié* and gliding it on the floor. To perform the *sissonne fermée de côté* without a change of feet, simply travel to the side in the same manner as for *dessus* and *dessous* but do not change the feet in closing.

Sissonne fondue (see-sohn fohn-DIU). *Sissonne* sinking down. The *sissonne fondue* is similar to the *sissonne fermée* but it is performed larger with a higher jump. In closing the step the second foot does not glide on the floor but is gently placed down in the fifth position, or placed *sur le cou-de-pied* so that the finish is on one foot. Like the *sissonne fermée,* the *sissonne fondue* may be performed *en avant, en arrière,* and *de côté* in any given direction in space.

Sissonne ouverte (see-sohn oo-VAIRT). Open *sissonne.* It is usually performed as a step of high elevation, *en avant, en arrière,* or *de côté,* finishing in any desired pose, such as *arabesque, attitude, croisé devant, écarté,* and so on. From the fifth position *demi-plié,* spring in the air, traveling in any desired direction; alight, *fondu,* on one foot, with the other leg raised in any given pose. *Sissonne ouverte en développé* is performed the same way, except that the raised leg is opened with a *développé* movement.

Sissonne ouverte en tournant (see-sohn oo-vair-tahn toor-NAHn). Open *sissonne* turning. From the fifth position *demi-plié,* spring into the air, turning *en dehors* (in the direction of the front foot); alight on one foot, opening the other leg with or without a *développé* to any desired pose.

Sissonne retombée (see-sohn rih-tohn-BAY). *Sissonne* refalling. See *Sissonne doublée.*

Sissonne simple (see-sohn SAN-plih). Simple, or ordinary, *sissonne.* It may be performed *derrière* or *devant.* For *sis-*

108

sonne simple derrière, from the fifth position *demi-plié,* spring into the air, stretching both feet to point completely, while remaining in the fifth position; alight *sur place* on the front foot, *fondu,* with the back foot raised to point *sur le cou-de-pied derrière.* For *sissonne simple devant,* reverse the above, finishing on the back foot with the front foot raised. It may also be performed with a change of feet in which case it is called *sissonne simple passé en avant,* or *en arrière.* Also called *temps levé* (Cecchetti method).

Sissonne simple détournée (see-soh*n* san-plih day-toor-NAY). Simple *sissonne* turned aside. From the fifth position *demi-plié,* spring into the air, turning a complete turn in the direction of the back foot *(en dehors)*; alight on the front foot, with the back foot raised to point *sur le cou-de-pied* either *derrière* or *devant.*

Sissonne simple en tournant (see-soh*n* san-plih ah*n* toor-NAH*n*). Simple *sissonne* turning. From the fifth position *demi-plié,* spring into the air, turning one complete turn in the direction of the front foot *(en dehors),* alight on the back foot, *fondu,* with the front foot raised to point *sur le cou-de-pied devant.*

Sissonne soubresaut (see-soh*n* soo-brih-SOH). *Sissonne* jerked. See *Temps de poisson.*

Sissonne tombée (see-soh*n* toh*n*-BAY). *Sissonne* dropping down or falling. A compound step consisting of a *sissonne simple* and a *tombé.* Also called *sissonne tombante* (Cecchetti method).

SIX (sees). Six.

SOUBRESAUT (soo-brih-SOH). Sudden jump, jolt, or jerk. From the fifth position *demi-plié,* spring into the air in the fifth position, with the legs tightly crossed and feet pointed. Alight simultaneously on both feet, *fondu,* without changing feet. It is usually performed traveling forward, *croisé devant* or *effacé devant,* with a backward lean of the body. It may, however, also be performed *sur place.*

Soubresaut, grand (grah*n* soo-brih-soH). Large, sudden jump. From the fifth position *demi-plié,* spring into the air, drawing the feet up with the toes pointing, knees bent, and one foot in front of the other. The position in mid-air is comparable to *grand plié* in the fifth position. Alight simultaneously on both feet, *fondu,* in the fifth position without changing feet.

SOUSSUS (soo-sIU). Literally, under-over. A springing *relevé* to a tight fifth position *sur les pointes* or *sur les demi-pointes.* It may be done *sur place* or traveling in any given direction forward or backward. Also called *temps de cou-de-pied.*

SOUTENU (soo-teh-NIU). Sustained, as in *assemblé soutenu; battement soutenu.*

SOUTENU EN TOURNANT (soo-teh-niu ah*n* toor-NAH*n*). Literally, sustained in turning. A turn on both feet, *sur les pointes* or *sur les demi-pointes,* taken from a *demi-plié.* It may be performed *en dedans* or *en dehors,* with a whole turn or a half turn. For *en dedans,* from the fifth position *demi-plié,* extend the back foot to the second position, remaining in the *demi-plié;* execute a *demi-grand rond de jambe à terre en dedans,* turning the body inward in the direction of the movement; close the working foot to the fifth position front, simultaneously springing to the *demi-pointes* or *pointes* and facing the back of the room; complete the turn on both feet finishing *de face.* For *en dehors,* reverse the above movements. See *Assemblé soutenu en tournant.*

SPOTTING. The technique of using the eyes in turning in

order to prevent dizziness in multiple turns, to maintain the equilibrium of the body, and to give a quality of brilliance to the turn. The theory of spotting is to focus the eyes on a definite spot at eye level, to maintain this focus as the body begins to turn so that the head lags behind the body, and then to turn the head rapidly before the body, and refocus the eyes, almost instantly, on the same spot, looking over the other shoulder as the body completes the turn.

SUITE, DE (dih sweet). Literally, continuously. A term used to indicate that a step or movement is to be repeated in continuity a number of times, as in *assemblés de suite*.

SUJET (siu-zhay). Person. A soloist of the company. *Sujet* is always qualified by *second, premier,* or *étoile*. A *second sujet* is a soloist of the second class; a *premier sujet,* soloist of the first class; *sujet étoile,* star soloist (French school).

SUR (siur). On, upon.

TABLEAU (tah-blo). Literally, picture. Artistically arranged groupings that form a large picture unit on the stage.

TAQUETÉ (tah-keh-tay). Literally, pegged. The *pizzicato* or *staccato* type of movement of certain steps danced *sur les pointes;* these movements are quick, small, precise, close together, and strike the floor lightly and sharply, digging into the stage. The *pas de bourrée piqué* is an example.

TEMPS (tah*n*). Literally, time. The word *temps* is here best defined as "movement." Its derivation is from a musical use of the word, which refers to the timing of a step to a rhythmical pattern.

TEMPS DE COU-DE-PIED (tahn de koo-dih-pee-AY). Literally, time of the instep, or movement of the instep. See *Soussus*.

TEMPS DE CUISSE (tahn dih KWEES). Literally, time of the thigh, or movement of the thigh. A compound step consisting of a *battement dégagé* and a *sissonne fermée*. It may be performed *dessus, dessous, en avant,* and *en arrière*. For *dessus,* from the fifth position *demi-plié,* execute a *battement dégagé dessus* with the back foot on the "and" beat of the measure, remaining in the *demi-plié,* and follow immediately with a *sissonne fermée de côté* in the direction of the back foot. For *dessous,* from the fifth position *demi-plié,* execute a *battement dégagé dessous* with the front foot on the "and" beat of the measure, remaining in the *demi-plié,* and follow immediately with a *sissonne fermée de côté* in the direction of the front foot. For *en avant,* from the fifth position *demi-plié,* execute a *battement dégagé dessus* with the back foot, remaining in the *demi-plié,* and follow immediately with a *sissonne fermée en avant*. For *en arrière,* from the fifth position *demi-plié,* execute a *battement dégagé dessous* with the front foot, remaining in the *demi-plié,* and follow immediately with a *sissonne fermée en arrière*. The body may be turned in any given direction.

TEMPS DE FLÈCHE (tahn dih FLESH). Literally, time of the arrow, or movement of the arrow. There are several variations of this step. In general, the first leg is supposed to represent the bow, and the second leg the arrow that shoots out. 1. From the fifth position *demi-plié,* with the back foot execute an *enveloppé* while springing into the air; at the moment when the toes of the working foot come in to the knee of the supporting leg, quickly raise the knee and *développer* the second foot sharply to *effacé devant,* while alighting *fondu* on the first foot. 2. From the fifth

112

position *demi-plié,* execute a *grand battement* with the front foot, *raccourci,* and spring into the air; quickly *développer* the second foot alighting *fondu* on the first foot. 3. From the fifth position, *grand battement en fondu,* spring into the air, changing feet with a second *grand battement,* the legs passing each other in the air. Also called *saut de flèche.*

TEMPS DE L'ANGE (tah*n* dih LAH*n*zh). Literally, time of the angel, or angel's movement. A soaring step similar to the *temps de poisson,* except that the legs are bent as in the old paintings of angels. The back is arched, the arms are in the fifth position, high, with the head back and leaning toward the arm nearest the audience.

TEMPS D'ÉLÉVATION (tah*n* day-lay-vah-sYo*n*). Literally, time of elevation. A generic term for all steps that involve jumping, springing, or leaping; for example, *changements, assemblés, jetés, sissonnes,* etc.

TEMPS DE POINTES (tah*n* dih PWAH*n*t). Literally, time of the *pointes,* or movements on the toes. The generic term for steps and movements performed *sur les pointes.*

TEMPS DE POISSON (tah*n* dih pwah-soH*n*). Literally, time of fish, or fish's movement. A type of *soubresaut.* From the fifth position *croisé, demi-plié,* spring high into the air with both feet, throwing them back in a well-crossed fifth position in the air. At the same time, raise both arms to the fifth position, high, and forcefully arch the back. At the instant of jumping, the body turns to *effacé* direction. Finish by alighting, *fondu,* on the front foot. Also called *sissonne soubresaut, soubresaut poisson,* and *pas de poisson.*

TEMPS LEVÉ (tah*n* leh-vAY). Literally, time raised, or raising movement. The raising of the body by means of an upward spring into the air from one foot or both feet.

Temps levé on one foot is a hop in which the jumping foot must forcefully push the floor away and extend itself fully into a stretched and arched position while the knee straightens completely. The *temps levé* finishes in a soft *fondu.* The raised foot may be in any given position—*sur le cou-de-pied, à la seconde, en arabesque,* and so on—or it may make a movement such as *fouetté* or *rond de jambe.* When the jump is taken off both feet to finish on one foot it may be called *sissonne simple* (French and Russian schools). *Temps levé* may also be performed *en tournant.*

TEMPS LIÉ (tahn lee-AY). Literally, time linked or linking movements. A series of co-ordinated movements involving the feet, legs, body, arms, shoulders, and head, which is one of the oldest steps in the ballet repertoire, originating in the dances performed at the French court. Today it is one of the most frequently used exercises of center practice, utilized to develop co-ordination, balance, and control, in changing the weight from one foot to the other, and from one position to the other, smoothly and rhythmically. The *temps lié* has a number of variations. It may be performed *simple,* at 90° with *développés* and *fondus,* and with *pirouettes,* to two-quarter or three-quarter time. In its simple form it has two variations.

En avant: 1. (two-quarter time) From the fifth position, *croisé* direction, with the arms in the fifth position *en bas. Demi-plié* and *chassé en avant* to the fourth position *pointe tendue croisé derrière,* at the same time raising the arms to the third position *en haut;* close behind to the fifth position *demi-plié,* lowering the raised arm to the third position *en avant; chassé à la seconde* with the front foot, finishing (*de face*) with the other foot *pointe tendue* to the second position; at the same time open the arm to the second position and turn the head to look at the hand; close the pointing foot front in the fifth position *demi-*

114

plié, lowering both arms to the fifth position *en bas.* Repeat, alternating sides as many times as desired. To perform the *temps lié simple en arrière,* reverse the movements. 2. (three-quarter or two-quarter time) From the fifth position, *croisé,* with the arms in the fifth position low: *Demi-plié* and extend the front foot *pointe tendue croisé devant* simultaneously raising the arms to the fifth position front, *demi-plié* in the fourth position equalizing the weight over both feet, retaining the arms in their position, straighten both knees, pointing the back foot to *croisé derrière* and simultaneously raising the corresponding arm to the third position high, close feet to the fifth position, retaining the arms in their position; *demi-plié,* and extend the front foot *pointe tendue à la seconde,* simultaneously lower the raised arm to the third position front, *demi-plié* in second position, equalizing the weight over both feet and retaining the arms in their position, transfer the weight to the side of the working foot stretching the opposite foot to *pointe tendue à la seconde,* simultaneously opening the arms to the second position, close foot *devant* in the fifth position, lowering arms to the fifth position low. Repeat all on the other side. Repeat on alternating sides as many times as desired. To perform *en arrière,* reverse the movements.

TEMPS PLANÉ (tah*n* plah-NAY). Time soared, or soaring movement. Also called *temps de l'ange.*

TENDU (tah*n*-DIU), **TENDUE** (tah*n*-DIU). Stretched, as in *battement tendu; pointe tendue.*

TERMINÉ (tair-mee-NAY). Ended or concluded, as in *pirouettes sur le cou-de-pied terminé en arabesque fondue.*

TERRE, À (ah TAIR). Literally, on the ground. 1. A term used to indicate that the supporting foot, or feet, are flat on the floor (*pied à terre*). 2. A term used to indicate that a pose which usually requires a lifted leg is to be performed with the extended foot remaining on the floor, as in *pointe tendue à terre; arabesque à terre.*

TERRE, PAR (pahr TAIR). Literally, by the ground. Same as *à terre.*

TIGHTS. See *Maillot.*

TERRE À TERRE (tair ah TAIR). Literally, ground to ground. Steps that are performed close to the floor with very slight elevation are called *terre à terre* steps; for example, the *glissade* and the *pas de basque glissé.*

TÊTE (teht). Head. See *Positions of the head.*

TIRE-BOUCHON, EN (ahn tihr boo-SHOHn). Literally, in a corkscrew, or in a corkscrewlike movement. A *pirouette en dedans* with a *renversé* movement, *pirouette renversée en tire-bouchon.* The *demi-plié* and upsetting movement of the *renversé* in turning give the impression of a corkscrew.

TOMBANT (tohn-BAHn). Falling down, for example, *sissonne tombante.* Also called *tombé.*

TOMBÉ (tohn-BAY), **TOMBÉE** (tohn-BAY). Literally, fallen down; falling. The movement of falling forward, backward, or sideways onto the working leg with a *fondu* from a raised position.

TONNELET (toh-neh-LAY). Literally, little cask. A short skirt stretched over a light hoop-shaped frame worn by male dancers of the eighteenth century.

TOUR (toor). Literally, turn. A turn of the body, as in *tour en l'air.* See *Pirouette.*

TOUR DE BASQUE (toor dih BAHSK). Literally, turn of the Basque. A type of *pas de basque* performed *en tournant.* From the fifth position *demi-plié,* execute a *demi-rond de* *jambe en l'air, en dehors à la demi-hauteur* with the front foot; spring onto the foot *sur la demi-pointe,* immediately closing the other foot in front in the fifth position *demi-pointes,* turning the body one-quarter turn; make a sharp continuation of the turn on both feet, finishing *de face* with a *coupé dessous.* Also called *piqué enveloppé* (French school).

TOUR DE FORCE (toor dih FORS). Literally, turn of strength. A virtuoso technical feat. A display of brilliance and strength in a difficult combination of steps, jumping, beats, or turns.

TOUR DE REINS (toor dih RIHn). Literally, turn of the loins. See *Coupé jeté en tournant* and *Jeté en tournant.*

TOUR EN L'AIR (toor ahn LAIR). Literally, turn in the air. A virtuoso step of the male dancer. A *changement* (or *soubresaut*) *en tournant* made with a single, double, or triple turn, depending on the skill of the dancer. From the fifth position *de face, demi-plié,* spring upward into the air with the feet well crossed in the fifth position; at the top of the jump turn the whole body forcefully into the desired number of turns (performed *en dehors* or *en dedans*) and alight *fondu* in the fifth position, with or without a change of feet. *Tour en l'air* may also end by alighting in a pose such as *arabesque* or *attitude* or by dropping onto one knee.

TOUR JETÉ (toor zheh-TAY). A commonly used corruption of the term *grand jeté en tournant.*

TOURNANT, EN (ahn toor-NAHn). Literally, turning. A term used to indicate that a given step is to be performed with a turn of the body, as in *pas de bourrée en tournant.*

TOURNÉ D'ADAGE (toor-nay dah-DAZH). Literally, turning of adagio movement. A rotation of the body from the fourth position front, or the second position, to *arabesque,* or vice versa, performed slowly as part of the *adage* exercise.

TOURNER (toor-NAY). To turn.

TOURS, CHAÎNÉS (sheh-nay TOOR). Literally, chain of turns. Also called *petits tours* and *déboulés.* See *Chaînés, tours.*

TOURS, PETITS (p'tee TOOR). Literally, small turns. See *Chaînés, tours.*

TRAVESTI, EN (ahn trah-vehs-TEE). Literally, in disguise. The term used to indicate that a girl is dancing a boy's part, or a boy a girl's part.

TROIS (trwah). Three.

TROIS-QUARTS (trwah-KAHR). Three-quarters; for example, *trois-quarts de tour.*

TROISIÈME (trwah-ZYEM). Third, as in *troisième position, troisième arabesque.*

TUTU (tiu-TIU). A short petticoat or ballet skirt worn by a *danseuse.*

Tutu

118

𝒰

UN (uhn), **UNE** (iun). One.

𝒱

VAGANOVA, AGRIPPINA (ah-GRE-pi-nah vah-GAHN-oh-vah), 1879–1951. She was born in St. Petersburg, Russia, and graduated from the St. Petersburg Imperial Ballet school. She became a *ballerina* of the Maryinsky Theater in 1915, then began teaching at the State School of Ballet, Leningrad (formerly the Imperial Ballet school, St. Petersburg), in 1919. She recodified the Russian system of teaching. In 1930 she became Artistic Director of the Leningrad Kirov Ballet Company (formerly the St. Petersburg Maryinsky Ballet). In 1934 she became Director of the Leningrad Choreographic Technicum and published her world-famous textbook, *Fundamentals of the Classic Dance* (translated into English by Anatole Chujoy and published in New York in 1946). She received the title Honored Artist of the Republic and headed the Soviet Choreographic Technicum. In Russia she was regarded as the chief architect of the Soviet Ballet School and the Soviet ballet style.

VAGANOVA SYSTEM (vah-GAHN-oh-vah). The system of training devised by Agrippina Vaganova, based on her training and experience in the Imperial Russian Ballet. It is widely used in the Soviet Union.

VARIATION (vah-ree-ah-SYOn). Literally, variation. Any solo dance in a classical ballet. According to Beaumont, it is probably derived from the musical term "variation," the repetition of a theme in a revised or elaborated form. An example is the Lilac Fairy's variation in *The Sleeping Beauty.*

VIRTUOSO (VUR-tiu-oh-so). A performer who excels in technical ability.

VOLÉ (voh-LAY), **VOLÉE** (voh-LAY). Flown; flying, as in *brisé volé*.

VOLÉE, DE (dih voh-LAY). Literally, by flying. A term used to indicate that a specific step is to be done with a flying or soaring movement, as in *entrechat cinq de volée*.

VOYAGÉ (vwah-yah-ZHAY), **VOYAGÉE** (vwah-yah-ZHAY). Traveled; traveling. Progressing by a series of small hopping steps while holding a pose such as *arabesque*. For example, *arabesque voyagée*.

Z

ZUCCHI, VIRGINIA (vear-zhee-nee-ah TSOO-kee), 1847–1930. A famous Italian ballerina who was a pupil of Carlo Blasis. See *Russian school*.